Heroic Leaders
A Courageous Leader

By John D. Hanson

All content in this book was written solely by the author. While AI was used for ideation and outlines, John wrote every word.

Heroic Leadership is a work of nonfiction. Nonetheless, some names and personal characteristics of individuals and events have been changed in order to disguise identities. Any resulting resemblances to persons living or dead is entirely coincidental and unintentional.

Copyright 2024 © 7 Ways Menu, LLC. All rights reserved.

Table of Contents

Acknowledgements	4
Recommendations	6
Foreword	13
Introduction	15

Define

Chapter 1: Leadership	21
Chapter 2: Heroism	55

Engage

Chapter 3: Empathy	75
Chapter 4: Attitude	97
Chapter 5: Do	116
Chapter 6: Earn Trust	135
Chapter 7: Responsibility	156
Chapter 8: Story	171

Empower

Chapter 9: Equip	184
Chapter 10: Support	197
Chapter 11: Recognize	207

Become

Chapter 12: Authentic	225
Confident	
Coachable	
Courageous	
Abundant	
Embracing Change	
Chapter 13: The Ultimate Proof	247
Coming soon!	254
Bibliography	256

Acknowledgements

As I reflect back throughout my life, there have been many engaging, Heroic Leaders who made a significant impact. Dale, David, Ralph, Dan, Chip, Matt, Kyle, Ken, Tim, Richard, Tom, Mike, Anthony, Troy, Brian, John, Luke, Ken, Pat, Chaz, Rob, Doug, Suzy, Chris, Markus, David, Patrick, Randy, Lou, Greg, Ryan, Sheri, Jason, Scott, Tom, and Armando, specifically.

I'm deeply grateful to the countless thought leaders and authors who poured themselves into their books to improve my life, career, Leadership, growth, and achievements. Their authentic guidance and actionable insights have deeply enriched my life and my career.

To the most Heroic Leader I know – my dearest wife. I would not be the Man, the Husband, the Father, the Leader, the Believer, the Professional, the Entrepreneur that I am today without your faithful, diligent belief in me. Our children are blessed to have you as their mom. Our faithful friends are mightily impacted by your honesty, wisdom, diligence, and giving.

To my Heavenly Father Who loves me more than I can fathom, enough to bring me an overwhelming abundance of incredible people, resources, insights, gifts, and experiences. May He be glorified in all I say and do.

Recommendations

"If you've been waiting for permission to do your dream....you have it.

Now go do it." — Dr. Kary Oberbrunner, *Wall Street Journal* and *USA Today* bestselling author

"Leadership isn't just a matter of titles or experience—it's about intentional design, not default.

In Heroic Leadership, John D. Hanson shows that true Leaders engage their people with clarity, purpose, and action.

When you apply his principles, you'll attract and empower those who get it, want it, and have the capacity to make a meaningful impact in every area of life." -- Gino Wickman, Author of *Traction* & *Shine*, Creator of EOS®

"Heroic Leadership could not be timelier.

As Leaders, we need to build the type of company that helps employees be proud of the work they do and have an opportunity to live their best lives.

Hanson nails it." – John R. DiJulius, III, Bestselling Author of *The Customer Service Revolution*

"Leadership isn't about titles or resumes—it's about stepping up and taking a stand, even when it's uncomfortable. In Heroic Leadership, John D. Hanson challenges the idea of default leadership and calls for Leaders who design their influence with intention. This book equips you to break through fear, redefine heroism, and take decisive action to create meaningful impact in business and life." – Marcus Sheridan, Keynote Speaker, Author of *They Ask, You Answer*, Dang Good Fellow on LinkedIn

"Heroic Leadership doesn't happen by chance—it takes persistence and a willingness to grow beyond roles and expectations.

In *Heroic Leadership*, John D. Hanson reveals how Leadership and heroism come from deliberate actions, not labels or positions.

If you're ready to commit to the process and apply these powerful principles, you'll discover the tools to Lead with purpose and transform your world." – Armando Leduc, Owner, Leduc Entertainment, Podcast Host of *Spaghetti on the Wall*, Public Speaker

"John D. Hanson's *Heroic Leadership* challenges the idea that leadership is about titles.

Hanson takes it further, laying out actionable steps that make impactful Leadership accessible to anyone willing to put in the work.

This book hits home for business owners and Leaders who are serious about building trust, empowering teams, and Leading with purpose.

Hanson's approach emphasizes character-driven actions—empowering readers to Lead by design, not by default.

If you're ready to elevate your game and make a lasting difference, *Heroic Leadership* is a must-read." -- Ken "Mr. Biz" Wentworth, Fractional CFO, Business Strategist, Author

"The most effective Leaders don't Lead by accident—they Lead with purpose and vision. Leadership isn't just a role you step into; it's a responsibility to inspire growth and impact.

In *Heroic Leadership*, John D. Hanson reveals that by understanding the deeper essence of Leadership and heroism, you can become the kind of Leader who not only achieves results but also elevates the people around you, creating lasting change." – David Meltzer, Co-Founder Sports 1 Marketing, Consultant, Business Coach, Keynote Speaker, 3x Best Selling Author

"I love how John quickly dispels common misunderstandings about Leadership and, in short order, helps us understand what it truly means to be a Leader.

Not just any Leader, a Heroic Leader.

This world needs more Heroic Leaders with the capacity to Lead as God intended - in our families, communities, schools, churches, workplaces, government, media, and society at large.

This book teaches us how." -- Nicole Jansen, Founder of Leaders of Transformation

"Leadership is the courage to step up, inspire others, and create meaningful change.

It's about Leading with empathy, purpose, and intentional action.

In *Heroic Leadership*, John D. Hanson shows that anyone can unlock their Leadership potential and make a lasting, positive impact.

This book is a powerful guide for aspiring Leaders ready to step into their full potential and Lead with heart and purpose." – Markus Neukom, Leadership Consultant, Strategic Advisor, Thought Leader

"For anyone interested in practical, real life, people-driven Leadership, this book is a must read." -- Brian Lee, CSP, Founder and CEO, Custom Learning Systems Group Ltd.

"In the Bible, Jesus tells His disciples that Leaders should not exercise authority over people. Instead, whoever wants to become great must come alongside others as a servant.

My good friend John D. Hanson has exemplified this throughout his life, serving our country and local community with distinction and honor.

I have worked side-by-side with John to help people understand their purpose and help them fulfill their aspirations of entrepreneurship.

This book will equip others to understand how they can be Heroic Leaders and achieve their aspirations of making a difference in the world." – Chaz Freutel, Co-Founder of NOBLE; Managing Partner of We Buy Cars America; Co-Founder of Auto Butler; Founder of Get-U-Connected

"Leadership by default leaves people disconnected, but Leadership by design builds trust and purpose.

In *Heroic Leadership*, John D. Hanson offers practical insights for Leaders who want to go beyond roles and titles, fostering deeper relationships through kindness, recognition, and empowerment.

When Leaders engage with intention, they inspire their teams to grow, succeed, and create lasting impact together." – Michael Kainatsky, President of Alinea Sales Group; Head of Growth for House of Bricks

Foreword

One only comes across Leaders like John D. Hanson every so often, as intentional and as consistent as he has been in our interactions. I have learned much about Leadership over a lifetime in the civilian workforce, both before and after my military career. I was blessed to have great Leaders during my time in service as an Infantry grunt and a highly trained Special Forces Soldier and Green Beret. I have witnessed what outstanding Leadership looks like, what poor Leadership looks like, and all in between. Therefore, I am uniquely qualified to endorse John as a Leader and his book, *Heroic Leadership*.

John practices what he preaches. After reviewing his book, I couldn't help but notice that I have witnessed him applying the same practices and steps. Heroic Leadership is a choice and must become a honed skill through training and continuous learning. A Heroic Leader Leads by example, is highly intentional, and always goes in advance of others. They Lead by design and are genuinely empathetic. A Heroic Leader always exhibits a positive attitude, good character, and good judgment. They are trustworthy and responsible. They consistently empower others and model a grateful perspective. A Heroic Leader has the "do or do not" frame of mind. They always under promise and over-deliver.

The ladder of success has many rungs of failure on the way to the top. *Heroic Leadership* is an excellent guide for those serious about upping their Leadership game. It's a simple to follow process that everyone in Leadership positions should read and put into practice. I am honored and privileged to endorse both John D. Hanson as a Heroic Leader and his book as one of the premier resources on the topic of Leadership.

SFC(Ret.) Randy Nantz

Special Forces Communications Sergeant, Green Berets

Adaptive Athletes Trainer & Mentor; Author; Podcast Host

Introduction

You're wrong about Leadership. You're also wrong about Heroism.

You're wrong about what they are, how to best achieve them, and who they're for.

If you've already got Leadership & Heroism figured out, or so you think, this book is not for you.

If you're not interested in Leadership or Heroism, this book is definitely not for you.

If you're not willing to put in the work, longer than you think it will take, then this book is not for you.

But....

If you're willing to take a fresh look at what Leadership and Heroism are, setting aside what you've **thought** they are, for perhaps your entire life, this book may be for you.

If you're willing to put in the work for longer than you think it will take, and trust the process, this book may be for you.

If you want to make a difference in the world, truly, and you're willing to put in the work, and you're coachable, and you're willing to trust me, this book is definitely for you.

You can have Leadership or Heroism by default, or you can achieve them by Design.

For the vast majority of my life, I had Leadership and Heroism by default. Perhaps I performed better than others or my younger self in those default roles, but never to what my full potential was.

In 2019, everything changed for me.

I added a business mentor. I intentionally invested into my self-education. I began pursuing highly specific, Big Hairy Audacious Goals (BHAGs). More importantly, I discovered what Leadership and Heroism actually were.

Is that when I became phenomenally successful, when everything went perfectly according to the plan? Absolutely not.

To all outward appearances, my life consisted of one major setback after another, one major failure after another.

But in those extremely challenging times, I learned invaluable truths about myself, about identifying & seizing opportunity, about the power of key relationships, and what Leadership and Heroism by Design look like.

It turns out that so many of the views and beliefs I had on Leadership and Heroism were wrong. These errors were reducing my positive impact & influence on others, and my income, as well as what I desired to provide for my loved ones.

When I began to share this incredible paradigm shift on what Heroic Leadership is and how accessible it is to anyone, one audience after another left our time together with a positive energy. There was a buzz in the room, as one person after another had a lightbulb moment where they realized that they too could be Heroic Leaders.

Heroic Leadership is not limited to someone's role or responsibilities, someone's career field, nor their experience, age, education, or upbringing.

But just because someone **says** they want to be a Leader, does not make them one. Just as someone who relies on their role, responsibilities, industry, experience, age, or education is not guaranteed to be an effective, let alone Heroic, Leader.

Through this book, I intend to encourage and equip anyone who desires to genuinely make a difference in their world, to increase their positive influence & impact on others' lives, and to achieve their income goals.

As I do in all of my books, I start with the definition of the words and their origin. Not what I think they mean, not what respected thought leaders say they mean, not even what is commonly accepted, but what the **actual definitions and origins are**. Then introduce proven approaches to effectively improve those qualities.

I fully believe that anyone who is willing to learn, believe, and execute can be a Heroic Leader.

Thank you for believing in me by getting this book. Take action on the powerful truths I will share with you.

This book will change your life and the lives of all those around you. You will become a Heroic Leader and change your world.

Define

Chapter 1

Leadership – What It Really Is

Leadership, what it really is

The vast majority of people in life lead by default, especially because of their roles: managers, business owners, executives, parents, teachers, and more. I state this with such certainty, because I saw this in myself for the vast majority of my life. I've also experienced this across every industry that I've worked within, consulted with, or spoken to, including the military, nonprofit, manufacturing, logistics, education, healthcare, finance, and technology.

The primary goal of this book is not to point fingers or to assign blame. I want to inspire and encourage people and professionals in every industry around the world. Once we understand what Leadership actually is, how accessible it is, and how to engage effectively through it, anyone can have life-changing impact on the people around them.

I want to help people who want to make a difference in the world.

What do I mean by default? For most of my life, I believed that Leadership was the role I earned, or the influence or impact I had on others. Those are aspects of Leadership, but not Leadership itself. What occurred in me, because of this misunderstanding, was that I put too much confidence in my responsibilities, my title, or my achievements.

In some instances, I **demanded** respect and commitment to my ideas and priorities. Part of what was confusing is that my hard work ethic, my diligence, my innovation, and my ownership mindset led to increasing responsibilities and management roles.

By all appearances, I was an effective Leader, growing in influence and impact.

But far too often, that confidence was a projection. I was *acting* how I believed Leaders should act. I was treating others as I believed Leaders should. I was expecting loyalty, diligence, and excellence from the people I was responsible for.

But I was wrong.

In 2019, I began a journey of self-discovery. This process included adding a business mentor, studying a variety of highly respected thought leaders, and researching the definitions and origins of high value words.

Leadership was one of those words. And what I discovered changed my life.

There are so many ideas about Leadership; it can be overwhelming: books, courses, TED-style talks, YouTube videos, masterminds, and conferences. I began reading and studying Leadership in my early 20's.

Thought leaders like John Maxwell, Simon Sinek, Brene Brown, Jim Collins, John DiJulius, Gino Wickman, Horst

Schulze, Malcolm Gladwell, Bob Burg, Liz Wiseman, Seth Godin, and Jocko Willink all contributed greatly to my personal and professional growth on the topic of Leadership. I'm incredibly grateful for the input of these genuine, authentic, caring influencers.

"Surely you're not saying that those respected, knowledgeable, experienced thought leaders are wrong about Leadership, are you, John?!"

Yes and No. Their content, advice, and experiences about Leadership are invaluable. But Leadership is not what we do or even how we do it. It's something else.

I asked myself two questions: "What do the words 'Leadership' and 'Heroism' mean, and where do they come from?"

The answers changed my life and my perspective, leading to one of my most highly demanded presentations, Heroic Leadership.

Where did I discover these life-changing paradigm shifts?

The dictionary. If you've read any of my books, you know I spend a lot of time referring back to the dictionary. Rich, meaningful words contain such power. I love to explore all the definitions of these key words and their origins.

The literal definition for the word Leadership is: "the capacity to Lead." The suffix "ship" means capacity.

This may not seem like an incredible discovery, so let's unpack this.

Because Leadership is the ***capacity*** to Lead, this means that Leadership is potential, opportunity. It's flexible, unlimited, open, and available to all. It doesn't matter what your age is, what your experiences are, what your education is, or what your current responsibilities are. ***Anyone*** can increase their capacity to Lead others.

Using a word picture, your capacity to Lead others could be a shot glass, or it could be a 5-gallon bucket. ***You determine which one it is.***

Leadership is entirely on you. Your capacity to Lead others is directly and powerfully driven by how you perceive Leadership, how you invest into yourself, and how you look for ways to continuously improve as a Leader.

This is one reason I believe there was such positive energy whenever I presented Heroic Leadership. Regardless of the industry -- white collar versus blue collar, healthcare versus skilled trades, administration versus operations -- everyone has the potential to be a highly effective Leader.

So what does the word "Lead" mean? That was the next question I asked myself, after realizing that Leadership is ***the capacity to Lead***.

"Lead" is a beautiful Old English word that I phrase as "bringing others along as someone who has gone before."

You'll notice that nowhere in this definition does it mention age, experience, role, gender, achievements, education, upbringing, training, or circumstances. None of them.

The inspiration for the subtitle of my book came from the delightful movie, *Ratatouille*. The famous chef Gusteau authored a book entitled, "Anyone Can Cook."

In the same spirit, I believe anyone can be a Leader, and a Heroic Leader at that.

Far too many people are leaders by default, or completely unaware that they are actually Leaders, and that they have the ability to expand their influence and impact.

What are some examples of leaders by default who may be completely unaware of this opportunity?

Older siblings, team members that have been with the company for longer than newly onboarded employees, peers, those who Lead by example - hard workers, best friends, respected family members, and more.

But there's a dark side to leading others. Sadly, there are toxic leaders by default in our personal and professional lives. They negatively influence and impact the people around them. They bring others along, but not in a positive way, not with encouraging words, nor examples of how things have worked well.

Tragically, I have seen promising organizations severely impacted by toxic team members or managers. Most likely, those people did not start off interacting with others that way. Difficult things in their past, their upbringing, their careers, or their setbacks changed them and their perspective on life. These unseen traumas, hurts, losses, or challenges can result in a person who negatively leads others.

And that's the first type of Leader. As I reflected on types of Leaders throughout my career, as well as in my own life, I identified 7 categories. While not a definitive list, these cover the vast majority of what I've observed in my life and in others.

1. Toxic
2. Unaware
3. Disengaged
4. Formulaic
5. Underequipped
6. Engaged
7. Heroic

I use word pictures often, because it's easier for me to communicate effectively what's on my mind. Einstein said that if you can't explain it to a six-year-old, you do not understand it well enough yourself.

I'm not saying that you all are six-year-olds! Far from it! The simplest concepts stick in our minds far better, and we take more decisive actions on things we fully understand.

So throughout this chapter, let's use the analogy of a tour guide to explain the 7 types of Leaders. After describing what these types of Leaders look like, I will share some ideas on how to positively address areas for improvement.

Toxic

Let's start with a toxic leader. This is the tour guide who hates their job. Why they decide to continue to show up for work is often only because of the paycheck or the negative influence they have on others. Clearly, they do not enjoy it, and that directly affects the guests on the tour. They aren't going to enjoy the experience either!

True, the guests all get through the tour, make all the stops, hear all the information they need, but it's not a positive experience. And they won't be back!

Toxic leaders, whether they're the owners of the business, senior managers, or tenured team members, all have the same effect eventually -- promising team members and valuable clients are driven away. The last thing an organization of any size or industry needs is to lose promising team members and satisfied customers.

Obviously, the privately held company run by a toxic leader won't fire the toxic leader -- themselves. I haven't seen that one before! Usually in business, if an owner is toxic, the situation resolves itself. If the owner will not change, their business will only serve other toxic people or be severely limited in its revenue and potential.

But it's the toxic, tenured team members who are the greater issue. In today's highly competitive workplace and marketplace, companies cannot afford to be impacted by churn – the consistent loss of team members and clients.

So why do organizations keep toxic team members? The reasons I've seen for keeping a toxic tour guide on staff are: misplaced loyalty, loss of tribal knowledge, difficulty to replace the role, an unwillingness to have difficult conversations, disconnected from the company culture, or are toxic themselves.

Disengaged

In this scenario, the tour guide is not the disengaged leader. It's the travel agent. The travel agent is the one who booked the trip for the tourists who will go on the experience with the tour guide. While travel agents do a remarkable job, they're not going on the tour with you. By no means am I speaking poorly of travel agents. I have several friends who are excellent at this. This is for example purposes only!

A travel agent type of leader says things like, "Here's what you need; let me know how it goes." They provide resources, ideas, best practices -- all good things. But they're not directly engaged with the process. They don't go on the tour; they don't experience the tour with the tourists. They're not involved.

Unaware

This is the tour guide who undervalues themselves, who doesn't realize the ability they have to make that tour experience exceptional. They may be young, inexperienced, have encountered too many negative tourists, or worked for difficult managers. Because of those experiences, they don't believe they can make a difference. They're likely to leave that job very soon, and perhaps quit being a tour guide all together.

Formulaic

These tour guides go through the motions. They do everything right, make all the stops, say the right script, check all the boxes.

But there's no enthusiasm. The tourists have an experience, but not an excellent one, not a memorable tour. On a scale of 1 to 5 stars, this would be a 3-star experience. OK. Average, normal, typical. But are most tourists happy with that kind of experience? Are they likely to book the tour again or recommend it to others? Not likely.

Underequipped

These are enthusiastic tour guides with bright, upbeat personalities. But they haven't done the work to learn all the details, nuances, or special aspects of the tour. So the tourists feel happy to go, but when they reflect later, they noticed that some details were missed. Underequipped, friendly Leaders can have a lot of people who like them. But that does not translate to impact and influence in making a difference in others' lives.

Engaged

This is the enthusiastic, highly knowledgeable tour guide. They know their stuff! The tourists could go on the same tour every year with this guide, and it would always be different, always better. This tour guide is always asking themselves, "How can I make this better?" They never settle for "good enough." These are the experiences that gain 5-star reviews and repeat tourists & referrals.

Heroic

We'll dive into deep detail on what Heroism is in the next chapter. But here's what a Heroic tour guide brings to the table.

Not only are they engaged and knowledgeable, but they add a level of intentionality and ownership to their role as a tour guide. Their goal is not only for the tourist to have a wonderful experience, they want to make a difference in the tourist industry. Their coworkers enjoy working alongside them. They earn exceptional tourist reviews. They're highly self-motivated, even having goals of owning or leading a tour company of their own.

Now, I want you to do something for me. In all 7 of these examples, I want you to change the words "tour guide" to "Leader" and "tourists" to "loved ones", "customers" or "team members."

Then ask yourself 2 questions: "What kind of tour guide or Leader am I?"; "How am I impacting the people around me?"

While being honest with yourself, also be truthful. We can be our toughest critics, so don't be too hard on yourself. Be honest AND truthful with yourself. Best of all, ask people you trust for their feedback.

Don't rush this self-assessment. These recommendations will not have high impact without a realistic, objective idea of where you stand as a Leader currently.

Recommendations for the 7 Types of Leaders

Toxic

It's highly unlikely that a toxic leader is going to be reading this book. My experience has been that they severely lack self-awareness, rarely look to improve on Leadership and culture, and often repeat the same patterns of missed opportunities, broken relationships, and under performance.

But let's say you work for a toxic leader. What are next best steps for you?

First of all, as difficult as it might be, I would encourage you to be looking for another opportunity. I know the age old saying that "zebras don't change their stripes" is overused, but the principle still applies. My experience has been that toxic people stay until the writing is on the wall that they will be fired. Most often, unfortunately, they remain on the team regardless of behavior, churn, avoidable mistakes, repeated errors, and costly poor decisions.

Why would you want to remain in that environment?

I'm not asking this question to be combative. If you truly feel that this is the place you should be because of the income, because of the commute, because of the lack of better options in your area, I understand. Perhaps you feel that you should remain with the company for the sake of other competent, committed colleagues. While commendable, I would take a serious look at this.

If you feel like you're settling for less, you probably are. In today's highly competitive workforce, the odds are exceptionally good that there is a quality company who would be thrilled to have you on their team. I know that there's risk involved in making a move to a brand-new company that has all the appearances of being better, when it could just be that the grass **appears** to be greener on the other side of the fence.

On the other hand, the risk of staying in a toxic environment negatively impacts more people than just you. It affects your coworkers, where they may think they have to put up with unacceptable behavior and culture. It affects your loved ones. The stress you're feeling at work unnecessarily can spill over into the lives of the ones you care for. And it definitely has a toll on you.

Should you choose to stay, I would highly recommend 2 things:

- 1) Invest intentionally and regularly into yourself. You cannot pour from an empty cup: at work, for customers, for colleagues, or for your loved ones. Regular self-care through exercise, hobbies, diet, sleep, laughter, and hydration should be diligently pursued.

Burnout doesn't mean you leave your job. Burnout means you're not the same person you were one year ago, two years ago, three years ago, and so on. You're not the same at work, you're not the same with your loved ones, and you're not the same towards yourself. No job is worth losing those things.

2) Intentionally pour into others. Step up your game of Leading others, especially the ones you know are hurting and believe that they should stay with the company, too.

They need your Leadership, and you need to strengthen your ability to impact and influence others. Because you desire to make a difference, this should be a top priority for you. It will also help you cope with the stress of being in a toxic work environment. When you're pouring into others, that helps you stay focused on making a difference, not just surviving.

If the tour company owner is toxic, seriously consider if you should be working for another tour company. There are plenty more out there.

On the personal side, if you have a toxic leader in your life, odds are that you can't easily separate yourself from them. You might be living in the same house!

So what can you do?

The advice is similar to those facing toxicity in the workplace….

1) Take the best care of yourself
2) Surround yourself with as many positive, encouraging, supportive friends as possible
3) Look for ways to pour into others, especially those who are also affected by the same toxic person

One of the clear traits of a Leader is a person who comes alongside those who are struggling to encourage and equip them. You'll be able to do this far more effectively if you are regularly engaging in self-care.

Disengaged

If you work for a disengaged leader, they may be unaware due to ignorance, or they may be choosing to remain unaware, so they don't have to deal with potentially difficult conversations or improvements. There's a fairly simple way to address this.

Ask if they're open to hearing suggestions for improvement. If they say no, then you know you're dealing with apathy.

Apathy can be more dangerous to a company than toxicity. No sense of urgency means no innovation, no hunger, no desire to grow or improve. Surviving versus thriving.

If you're seeking to be an Engaged, Heroic Leader, this work environment is not a good fit for you either.

On the other hand, if the owner of the tour company is simply unaware and responds positively to your input, wonderful! But there's a catch.

Awareness does not equal action.

Just because someone is now aware of things that need to be improved, does not mean that they're going to take action to improve them.

Do you know the difference between listening and hearing?

Hearing is a default ability that all of our bodies possess. Listening, on the other hand, especially active listening, is a choice -- a choice to receive, process, and respond to input.

The easiest giveaway if a Leader seeks to become engaged is what they do with the ideas, feedback, and input you share with them.

If you have to continually remind them, regardless of how kind their response may be, this proves that they don't believe your feedback is something they should act upon.

Our actions reveal our beliefs.

If a disengaged leader does not take action, it reveals that they believe everything is okay just the way it is.

I would encourage you to look for another company if this is the case.

If they take action on what you suggest, wonderful! Now you have the opportunity to be an Engaged, Heroic Leader, regardless of your role or experience, within the company. Not only will this affirm your commitment to making a difference, it will also encourage your colleagues to share their feedback as well. A tremendously positive ripple effect; well done!

It's far simpler to avoid a disengaged leader in our personal lives. Their outlook on life is not directly impacting our quality of life, should they choose not to listen to our input. And if they do hear what we're saying and take action, our relationship is improved.

Unaware

If you're reading this book, you're likely aware that you desire to be a person of influence and impact towards others, that you desire to be a Leader.

These ideas for the unaware Leaders are more pointed towards your colleagues who undervalue themselves. Using the tour guide company for an example, you could be the one who points out to a fellow tour guide that they have the potential to be an excellent tour guide. Whether you contribute to their learning, growth, and progress or not, if they respond positively to your encouraging words, that's another proof that you're an Engaged Leader. When Leaders inspire or equip other Leaders, that's one of the best proofs of Leadership.

Healthy organizations value these team members who look to encourage and equip their colleagues. Sometimes, simple forms of Leadership can be highly effective, bringing about significant positive change over time to a company. Imagine if you were the one responsible for that growth! How cool would that be?!

This would be especially rewarding if you help a friend or loved one in your personal life discover their Leadership potential. It's special to see the "light bulb come on," when they understand that they can be a Heroic Leader as well, regardless of age, experience, or other factors. Very cool!

Formulaic

This is also a challenging type of Leader to encourage. The ones going through the motions are receiving exactly what they want out of their experience: a paycheck, stability, purpose, routine. But they're usually not happy, fulfilled, or self-motivated to achieve more. "Good enough" is often their standard, in life and at work. It can be just as hard to positively influence a formulaic Leader, as it can be to support an apathetic one.

My recommendation would be to ask a few well-worded questions, to discover some clues as to why they're working in this way.

Questions like: "I'm curious - why did you start with our company" or, "What do you enjoy the most from your work here?," or, "Is there a goal you're shooting for while working here?"

These questions aren't meant to be nosy. You're trying to understand if this is someone who desires to progress in their career. Whether you're in a Leadership role currently, or desire to be one in the future for this company, it would be good to know what this person's motivators are.

If they respond with an apathetic or unclear answer, they are not ready to be "brought along" by you, to be led by you. And that's okay. Focus on the ones who are ready.

You're not likely to encounter a formulaic Leader in your personal life. Perhaps they're just going through the motions, in a default leadership role. Gentle questions work well for friends and relatives who may be struggling with a lack of purpose or clarity. Your well-worded questions may help them discover their potential.

Underequipped

If you ask any engaged Leader, they would much rather have an enthusiastic team member than an experienced one lacking in positive energy. Positive energy is an infectious thing, in a good way! You want your team to be full of energetic, innovative, creative people. As long as the underequipped Leaders are open to input, coaching, encouragement, and innovative ideas, they're highly likely to take your recommendations and run with them.

Look for people in your organization who are hungry, eager to learn, who want to make a difference like you do. If you've been with the company longer, you absolutely have the opportunity to equip these high energy, enthusiastic, bought-in team members.

Look for clues that they're highly self-motivated.

Do they pay close attention to all that's going on within the company? Are they always a little early rather than right on time? If the company offers training, do they consistently sign up? They tend to have a smile and a positive attitude. They're curious. They ask good questions. They seek to do excellent work and are disappointed if they don't achieve that. They're open to innovative ideas.

If you reflect back to when you were starting out in your career, do these qualities describe you? It's far easier for an underequipped, enthusiastic tour guide to become an engaged Heroic Leader. All that's lacking is more experience, fresh ideas, and the right people to come alongside them.

You could be the Heroic Leader they need.

How rewarding it would be to help a close friend or relative who is hungry to grow, improve and excel in life! You can be the catalyst for their growth. I know it can be more challenging to come alongside people who know you, but if you're seeing the clues that they're coachable and open to innovative ideas, go for it! You could be the one helping them grow to the next level. What a great feeling!

Engaged

These tour guides are easy to spot. Not only are they enthusiastic, but they're experienced and get results.

They're also quite rare. Because I possess an ownership mindset, I'm always looking for others who share the same desire for excellence, for growth, for innovation, for continuous improvement. They stand out, in a good way.

If this type of Leader resonates with you, either because of where you are currently in your career, or where you aspire to be, then these next chapters will be especially helpful for you, and for those you desire to influence and impact as well.

This is also quite true in our personal lives. Engaged Leaders are difficult to find. If you possess an entrepreneurial spirit, you're already in the minority. You might be the only one in your circle of friends or loved ones.

That's why it's especially important to surround yourself with like-minded people. Engaged friends and family are also easy to spot. They're the ones who sincerely listen to your ideas and support *you* – not your circumstances, not your results to this point, not your achievements. They believe in you, period.

If you have people like this in your life, let them know how much they mean to you. Then look for others in your friends or family that may need the same encouragement from you.

Heroic

There's one more level, higher than an Engaged Leader. By no means am I saying that Engaged Leaders are settling for less. It really depends on what your goals are in life and in your career, if pursuing Heroic Leadership is a great fit for you.

We'll unpack what Heroism looks like displayed through Leadership in the next chapter. For now, consider these attributes as one of the highest levels of Leadership, using the analogy of a tour guide company:

Heroic tour guides not only make a difference to their customers and their colleagues and their owners, but they have goals that extend beyond their current organization.

They desire to influence and impact a large number of people, personally, professionally, within the walls of where they work, and especially outside the company.

They aspire to significant impact and influence.

They don't limit their potential. They see their capacity for Leadership as something that's always growing larger. They probably started with a shot glass in capacity, and they're not content with settling for a 5-gallon bucket either.

If you've spent time with someone who has Heroic aspirations, settling for the 5-gallon bucket of impact and influence, to them, is like settling for a shot glass of impact when the Pacific Ocean of influence is possible.

Do you have dreams, aspirations, or BHAG's that are larger than most? If you do, it's highly likely that you have Heroic intentions.

If your highest goal is to be an Engaged Leader, excellent! The world, the workplace, and relationships desperately need engagement. Both of these aspirations make a difference in the world.

If you desire to make a difference in the world, whether that world is immediately around you, or far larger than you can possibly imagine, it does not matter.

It's not about the size of our impact as Leaders; it's about the intentionality.

If you're intentional about your capacity to Lead others, you *will* make a difference in the world.

You can be a Leader by Default or a Leader by Design. Let's design your Leadership journey!

Before we take a deep dive into the ways to be Engaged and Heroic Leaders, let's take a moment to discover what Heroism truly is.

Leadership – My Capacity to Lead

My Next Best Steps

_____

_____

_____

Chapter 2

Heroism – What It Really Is

Heroism – it's pulled at humanity since the beginning of time. It seems like every civilization in the world has had at least one hero.

In 2021, it struck me....what is Heroism?

No surprise! I went to the dictionary, and, just like every visit to Mr. Webster's book, my life was dramatically impacted by the seismic paradigm shift I experienced.

Heroism, according to Webster, is the pursuit of 2 qualities: Excellence and a Higher Purpose. If your thoughts immediately run to our go-to answers for likely candidates – the military, healthcare providers, devoted educators, first responders, those who serve people with developmental disabilities – that would make sense.

But, if I were to say, "What about you?"

"ME?!! Are you kidding?! I am definitely NOT a Hero!"

But why is that a ridiculous questions to ask?

The definition clearly states that: 1) if you desire to do your absolute best, to strive for excellence, 5 stars AND (2) you combine this life ethic with elevating others as more important than yourself, you ARE a Hero, literally.

Why does that seem so preposterous to us?

We've been conditioned to accept the idea that Heroism is reserved only for those professions I mentioned and Hollywood movies.

But that's not what the definition is.

And we unknowingly reinforce these assumed Heroic roles by automatically assigning Heroism to people in these roles.

Not every single soldier I served with in the military gave their absolute best or put others ahead of themselves. The same is true for people I've encountered in the other "automatically Heroic" industries.

What we do does not determine whether it's Heroic. That's Heroism by Default.

We all can pursue Heroism by Design.

Just like Leadership, we need to set aside what we've heard, what we've read, what we've been told, what even feels right to us.

The definitions and meanings of words carry tremendous potential.

Potential is only potent when it's pursued.

Similar to Leadership, Heroism does not rely upon role, experience, age, or gender. Forget about titles!

Focus on impact and influence.

Focus on adding value to others (a higher purpose) through your absolute best work (excellence).

Everyday heroes are all around us.

The story lines of popular movies reinforce the idea that ordinary people can take extraordinary action on the behalf of others.

That can be you!

It's actually proven that those who DO NOT have a title can have just as much positive impact on others as those in traditional Leadership roles.

But here's where the differentiator comes in....

Are we being Heroic by Default (or not at all) or by Design?

What if we chose, every day, to make a difference in the world around us? For our loved ones, for our colleagues, for our partners, for our communities.

Intention determines Impact & Influence.

There are plenty of thought leaders in the world who intend to impact & influence others....for their own gain.

That's not what I'm referring to. Their income, their following, and their fans is their reward.

Those who pursue excellence for the benefit of others are doing so because **it's the right thing to do.**

In a world that craves authentic Leaders who genuinely care for others, most people can tell when someone seems too good to be true. Ultimately, experiences over time will be the ultimate test of authenticity.

So how can we Heroically Lead others in authentic ways?

Here are 7 ideas.......

Endurance

You've probably heard the old saying, "When the going gets tough, the tough get going." It's true! Few things distinguish everyday Heroes better than pressing on, when difficulty comes along, when the plan is not working, when the task at hand is no one's favorite!

Remember the definition for Lead: "Bringing others along as someone who has been there before?" Those who have "been there, done that" tend to have greater endurance than those who are first timers.

This is where Heroism kicks in....

Regardless of your role, age, experience, education, or skills, when you step out of your comfort zone (doing nothing, staying in your lane, hoping someone else will step up) and into Heroism (helping others to keep going, coming alongside to support & encourage, putting others' and the team's success ahead of yours) you exhibit the finest qualities of Heroic Leaders.

Example

While this is the simplest way to Heroically Lead others, it's also one of the most effective. We DON'T want to be the ones who say, "Do what I say, not what I do."

In the military, I have seen lower ranking soldiers Lead Heroically, regularly surpassing the leadership of higher-ranking soldiers.

They weren't showing off or showing up the others. They saw what needed to be done, took initiative, and came alongside others to get the job done.

This is especially important when the task is dirty, boring, or menial.

That's when Heroic Leadership shines through. While Heroism is often associated with danger, I passionately believe that Heroic Leadership is best proven in the ordinary, dull, boring tasks that must be accomplished for the good of others.

Empathy

We'll dive into this attribute in greater depth in the very next chapter, so I'll just say that Empathetic Leaders can be the most effective Leaders, because they automatically think about others before themselves.

There is a danger to being an Empathetic Leader, I discovered. After working with care giving organizations, I realized why they tend to have an extremely elevated risk for burnout. More to come on that in Chapter 3....

Effort

It's hard to outwork a Hero.

When someone says that their grandfather or father was/is their Hero, that's not a stretch. Often, their hard work ethic was/is one of their character qualities that earned them such respect.

And rightly so.

But this quality also has a dark side to it. I have observed far too many hard-working men and women who devoted decades of their lives to a company, a cause, or a business of their own, only to reach the point where they can (or must) retire.

Sadly, their health, relationships, and dreams have been so severely damaged over the years that they're often not able to enjoy those "golden years."

Why is that?

Because they passionately believed that hard work equaled the right thing to do. If it was hard, miserable, unenjoyable work, then they were up to the task. Reminds me of sayings like, "If it was easy, everyone would be doing it" or "Whatever it takes…." or the simpler catchphrase, "Get 'er done!"

I was talking about the Western New York work ethic with a friend of mine. We were both born and raised in Rochester, New York. Rochester and Buffalo are known for their blue-collar, hard-working history. Before recording our podcast conversation, Marc shared a story about working on the rear deck of his house. He kept finding that the work was taking far more time and effort than he thought the job should take. He could have "soldiered on" and got the job done anyway.

But he didn't.

He paused to think about HOW he was building the deck, and an idea came to him that saved him time and effort.

The danger of an excellent work ethic is that sometimes we work harder and longer than necessary.

Yes, we should be setting a good example for those around us. But not at the expense of our health, happiness, and relationships.

Work harder, smarter, and wiser. Is it Win/Win truly?

While Heroism is selfless, it must never be one sided. The Hero should absolutely benefit from pursuing excellence for the good of others.

Don't "work yourself to death." That saying came from somewhere, didn't it?

Don't be a statistic.

Be a Difference Maker.

Education

Sounds like our school days, doesn't it? When I use the word "education," I simply mean teaching others. When we share best practices, what NOT to do, and proven strategies, we are educating others.

In this aspect of Heroic Leadership, HOW we educate others is critically important. It must always be to assist them in achieving what THEY want to accomplish. If they feel like we're talking down to them or trying to get them to do it our way, it will not be well received.

So how do we educate others without being condescending or controlling?

By asking questions.

If we can help them identify the next best step on their own, with a little bit of prompting or guidance, we will have taught them how to fish rather than giving them a fish, so to speak.

Guiding Discovery is far better than Giving Direction.

I'm deeply grateful for the lessons I've learned throughout my life from those who functioned as helpful guides.

Best Steps versus Bossing Around.

Which one would you prefer to work with?

Encouragement

In 2019, a dear friend named Pat helped me identify that my life purpose is to Encourage Others. Whether it comes through the form of a workshop, a keynote speech, a book, a 1-on-1 conversation, or business coaching, I am most fulfilled when I'm adding value to others by identifying what's true in their lives and building them up on that truth.

If only I had known this while I served in the military. It would have taken my impact and influence to a higher level. I did have meaningful impact on some soldiers, but it could have been to a Heroic level if I had been able to add value to any personality, working style, rank, or maturity level.

I'm convinced that the majority of people in the world are desperately in need of encouragement, not flattery or feeling good about themselves. Those things are manipulative, shallow, and do not last.

An encouraging word, on the other hand, can last for a lifetime.

In a future chapter, I'll share with you my incredible experience with Ralph.

If we fully appreciate how positive, affirming words can impact people for life, then Heroic Leadership is not a Hollywood script. It can be an everyday opportunity.

Seize it!

Excellence

Horst Schulze, the co-founder of The Ritz Carlton Hotel, wrote in his book, *Excellence Wins*, that there's always room at the top for excellence.

Always!

Customer service surveys prove this. Excellent service experiences are a single-digit percentage. The bulk of customer interactions fall to average, fair, or poor -- 3 stars or lower. That being said, the bar is set fairly low to achieve more-than-ordinary (extra-ordinary) experiences.

Why is this?

Don't most people and companies ***say*** they want to achieve 5 stars, to achieve excellence?

Ahhh, but saying you want to achieve excellence, and putting in the work to achieve it, are two vastly different things.

Imperfect action always tops perfect intent.

My good friend, Nick Glimsdahl, was a guest on my radio show, The Heroic Experience. The show ran for 2 seasons. Nick was a repeat guest because of his strong background and keen insights from the world of Customer Experience. I'll never forget one quote he shared with me:

"5-star Customer Experience is simple, but it's not easy. If it were easy, everyone would be doing it."

So true.

It's not the level of difficulty to understand what needs to be done. It's the diligent and consistent modeling, rewarding, reinforcing, and teaching of the habits that need to be in place to achieve excellence.

And this is where Heroic Leadership comes in....

Ritz Carlton set the standard in the hospitality world for 5-star service levels. Not by accident, but by intention.

In a later chapter, we'll dive into the ways they achieved consistent excellence around the world at every location.

Excellence is never an accident. It's an accomplishment.

Heroism – Excellence & a Higher Purpose

My Next Best Steps

_____

_____

_____

Engage

Chapter 3

Empathy

Gallup's Clifton Strengths identifies Empathy as a professional strength. I didn't know that until I read, *Now, Discover Your Strengths*, by Marcus Buckingham, who worked for Gallup for many years.

The most effective Heroic Leaders use Empathy to engage with their colleagues, team members, and customers. But what is it?

In a nutshell, Empathy is putting ourselves in others' shoes. It's The Golden Rule stated in a unique way – Do unto others **as they would have done unto them**. This is often called The Platinum Rule. I believe it explains the intent behind The Golden Rule. After all, the only way we can most effectively love our neighbor is to understand **how they prefer to be loved.**

I believe there are 4 typical responses to Empathy: unaware, against the grain, a learned skill, or it comes naturally.

What's so cool about Empathy is that it positively impacts others whether it comes naturally to us or not. When we authentically engage with others through Empathy, they can't tell whether we're well-trained or whether it comes naturally to us. And that's the whole point.

Empathy is one way we prove that we genuinely care for others, that we put others before ourselves.

Let me share a scenario with you to show how Empathy is or is not used by others in real life....

You're eating a tasty meal in a busy restaurant. The servers are hurrying from one table to the next, refilling drinks, clearing tables, or bringing the food to hungry diners.

All of a sudden, you hear a loud crash as a server drops a large tray of hot, delicious food.

What just went through your mind? How would you respond to that situation?

Here are the 4 typical responses:

1) You don't notice anything unusual and continue eating (unaware)
2) You consciously think about how the dropped food affected many people – the diners, the server, the store manager, other customers, the cooks in the kitchen. That's a learned response.
3) You immediately feel bad for all the people I mentioned above, as well as identifying with how they all must feel. You don't have to consciously think; you automatically feel for them, especially if you've been in those roles. That's when Empathy comes naturally to you.
4) As a server, this 4th response bothered me a great deal. Have you been eating out, heard a dish shatter, and noticed someone applauding?! That upset me when people would do that; so rude. Those

people are showing that Empathy goes against the grain for them. They likely thought it was funny.

How would you respond in this example?

That can help reveal how naturally you feel Empathy towards others or whether it's more of a learned, caring trait.

One word of caution: if you're an empathetic Leader or an Empath, it is not wise to carry other's concerns. You should be using Empathy as an effective tool when needed, not a default, ongoing response.

If an empathetic Leader or an Empath does not use Empathy, as a tool that can be set aside until the time it's needed next, then they risk burning out.

It's simply unsustainable to carry the burdens of so many people. That's why intentional, regular self-care is a necessity for empathetic Leaders or Empaths. They cannot pour from an empty cup. Genuine care for others requires that naturally Empathetic Leaders **must** take care of themselves in order to continue their high level of caring engagement.

For the remainder of this chapter, let's walk through some ways to intentionally practice Empathy towards others as a learned professional and personal skill.

Motivations

One exercise I highly recommend, especially for aspiring Leaders, is to discover their motivations. When the alarm clock goes off, while it's still dark outside, what gets you out of bed in the morning?

It's interesting to me that my attendance, quality of work, and health was far better when people were depending on me. There were many times in my career where the job was not ideal, not what I aspired to. And I still got up and went to work because of my loved ones.

So what are those motivators for you? This is an exercise I provide for a few of my workshops. I recall one instance in particular.

It was a Cleveland, Ohio area credit union. Local, with a few locations, they scheduled a half day workshop on customer service. I opened the workshop with this exercise to help better understand their world and the world of their customers.

The idea came from the lean manufacturing model that Toyota developed. If you want to find the root cause of an issue, rather than just fixing the symptom that keeps popping up time again, ask the question "Why?," five times.

Simon Sinek has excellent material entitled, *Start with Why*. It occurred to me that if I could ask myself and workshop attendees the question "Why?" five times, I could discover what was most important to us.

For this local credit union in greater Cleveland, I wanted all of us to understand why they had long-tenured team members and highly satisfied clients. They weren't the largest credit union in the area, and there were plenty of other banks in that region as well.

I wanted to know from them why they chose to stay with that smaller credit union. I asked them why it was important for them to stay. Then I asked, "Why is that important you?", five times.

We discovered that people stayed on that team because of a sense of belonging. Not benefits, not useful work, or a flexible schedule. They felt like they belonged, a highly emotional reason to remain on the team.

What about their customers? We didn't have any customers on hand that day to ask, so we projected what their answers would be. Again, we asked, "Why did they stay with your credit union versus another?," five times.

The 5th answer was that they trusted the credit union to protect their loved ones' future.

Trust and belonging. Not features or benefits, not interest rate or return, not banking hours, none of those things. Both emotional drivers – a sense of belonging and trust.

Take a moment, pause from reading this book or listening to it, and ask yourself, "Why is it important to you to do what you do, to be where you are?"

Ask yourself "Why is that important to you?" five more times. I do this exercise for myself often. Life changes. Who I was five years ago, let alone 10 years ago, is not the same person I am today. My life circumstances and my family have changed, along with several other factors.

Here's what I found interesting. I discovered I had a strongest motivator and a deepest motivator. My deepest motivator was my personal faith. Everything I do is based on that.

But my strongest motivator was my loved ones. I mentioned earlier that I was far more motivated for my work, my attendance, my quality, and my health, because my loved ones were depending on me. When the alarm clock went off early in the morning, it wasn't my personal faith that got me out of bed. It was my dedication to provide for my loved ones.

That's the difference for me between my deepest and my strongest motivators.

I think you will find this Why Exercise insightful as you work through your career path and as your close personal relationships develop over time.

It's fascinating to do this exercise for workshop groups, especially for the same company. They always get to a deeper motivator than what is on the surface.

I recall very clearly one workshop in the western United States, where a young man offered to be the "guinea pig" for the group. I discovered later that this man had a successful career in the United States Navy before joining this industrial company. Fascinating.

He started off by saying it was important to him to join this company because he felt like he belonged. When I asked him why that was, he responded that it was the first time in his career that he felt like he belonged. I was intrigued to see what his deepest answer would be, so we continued to ask the question "Why?" three more times. The deepest answer was that he was freed to do his very best work.

If you have people you continually work with, it could be quite interesting to help them learn more about themselves. You also learn more about them. Hardly any conversations at work get to this kind of depth. Of course, this can't be a conversation with just anyone. But if you have a good working relationship with someone, it can be insightful for both of you.

Once you understand the motivators of the people around you, it will enable you to have greater impact and influence.

Not just because you know more about them, but you know more than possibly anybody else in their lives. Genuine curiosity to understand their strongest, emotional motivators will differentiate you from just about everyone else. That's huge!

Passion

Passion can sound like an extraordinarily strong word. What I actually mean is what's important to you, what's important to the people around you. Yes, you could start with what they enjoy doing. That's a terrific way to connect, to find similarities, or to just learn more about someone.

So definitely ask them about what they enjoy doing - hobbies, what they like to watch or read, what do they enjoy learning, what they do to unplug.

You can also add value to them by connecting what's important to them. Because we are our toughest critics, we can underestimate how our quality work impacts the team.

When someone else authentically points out to them what's clearly important to them by their quality of work, positive attitude, hunger to learn and improve – they are enabled to see that **how** they do their work has significant impact on the overall success of the company.

As a Heroic Leader, you have the ability to encourage and inspire others in this way. Regardless of your role, experience, title, background, education, or experience, you can help bring out the best in others, by highlighting what they do very well, what they do intentionally well.

Purpose

More important than passion is our purpose. Most people underestimate the impact of what they do. Why they do quality work and how they do their work does matter. Far more people are depending on their quality work than they realize.

During another workshop out west in the United States, I was facilitating a full day training event for a group of HVAC professionals.

No matter what we do, over time, can feel like everyday work - one day blends in with the next. In this workshop, I highlighted the fact that a large number of people were depending on the quality of their work. Not just quality of life - whether a building is hotter than it should be or cooler than it should be - but critical environments like hospitals, schools, military bases, and other key facilities. Safety, health, and people's lives are at stake. Even something as simple as a major office building, with thousands of people working in it, by extension, those people represent thousands more.

By providing quality service, this HVAC company, by extension, preserves and protects the lives of 10,000's of people, perhaps hundreds of thousands.

You might be thinking to yourself, "I don't do one of those essential roles." That may be true. But your quality work contributes to the overall success of your company. Commit to doing your absolute best work, and the overall success of the company is far more likely.

You all make a difference. By reminding your coworkers that you all make a difference, you are being a Heroic Leader.

Acknowledge, Ask, Act

In 2013, I was downsized along with a few hundred other people at a Fortune 10 company. Our family really needed the benefits this company offered, so I worked as hard as I could to find a job within the company. I ended up securing a role at a contact center. We kept the benefits. The challenge was: I had never worked in a contact center before, and the pay was almost half of what I was making before. Lower pay, a stressful work environment, not a preferred career step – but I had to make the most of it.

Within 90 days, I was training new hires because my customer satisfaction, my compliance, my quality, and my issue resolution were the top of my team. I credit my natural ability to empathize as a key to my success.

More than half of my calls on a daily basis were for people who had issues, who had problems that needed to be solved. Anyone can handle a smooth transaction, in person or over the phone. But it takes skill to excel at working through difficult conversations. Here are some of the strategies I learned from that demanding role that I have used personally and professionally to this day.

Be like Teflon, the nonstick coating pans. The very first thing I had to do was to learn that their negative emotions were not directed at me. It couldn't stick to me. I needed to be like a nonstick pan. Those emotions couldn't affect my customer service for them.

On the other hand, I could not ignore the emotions of the situation. As tempting as it was to jump right to the solution, I realized that I needed to address the emotion on the other end of the phone. I had to acknowledge that it was frustrating for them. Just a few words, but stating them with a genuine attitude. You've had experiences where you were calling for service of some kind, and you could tell the person was reading from a script. Or that they didn't genuinely have concern for your issue. It comes through the phone, doesn't it?

Expressing genuine concern while also assuring them that I would work with them to find a solution to their issue. This is a tremendous life skill for Heroic Leaders to possess.

Next phase - asking well worded questions. John Maxwell authored an insightful book entitled, *Good Leaders Ask Great Questions*. One idea from the book strongly resonated with me: The quality of the answer is dependent upon the quality of the question. The better questions we ask, the better answers we get.

I learned how to ask questions, and I learned how to do it in an efficient manner. As you may know, phone-based customer service agents are timed. (I know, I know –

Zappos was the rare exception, where they were encouraged to stay on the phone longer!) Phone-based service agents are tasked with taking care of the issue as quickly as possible, a measurement called Average Handle Time, or AHT.

We literally had a ticking clock showing us how long our phone call was going. While it was tempting to jump right to fixing what they needed, asking just a few well worded questions made sure I took care of everything they needed, not just the most obvious issue.

We were not just measured on how long the call took, along with saying the right words exactly, we were also measured as to whether we took care of their issue on the very first call, known as First Call Resolution, or FCR.

Acknowledging emotion lessened handle time because it enabled me to get to resolving their issue faster. Asking well worded questions enabled me to solve the root cause or address multiple concerns in one phone call. This ability can work well in any industry, in any size company, for any role.

But there's one more element that's critically important – taking action. Most often, I could solve customers' issues on my own. Occasionally, I needed to get a supervisor's authorization or work with another department. Either way, I would need to connect that caller with a third party.

The faster way to do that is to simply transfer the phone call, known as a cold transfer. Simply forwarding the call to the next party saved quite a few seconds from the total call time.

But have you called in for service support and gotten disconnected during the transfer? If your call gets lost in the black hole of technology, that does not solve the problem. If that person calls in again, are they less upset, the same, or more upset? A rhetorical question, I know. They are more upset. That's why I chose to always provide warm transfers. Before thinking this doesn't apply in your world, listen just a little bit longer.

Let's say a credit card holder had a fraudulent transaction on their statement. I couldn't take care of that for them; they needed to speak with our Fraud Team. To make sure they got connected, I would conduct a warm transfer. Here's what that looked like.

I would tell the caller, "I'm going to connect you with our Fraud Team now. I'm going to stay on the line with you when we connect with the Fraud Team. I'm going to introduce you and provide a summary of what we talked about to my colleague."

Several seconds later, we would be connected; I would introduce them and explain what we needed help with.

Yes, it cost me time to do that. But the issue was resolved on the first call, the customer was highly satisfied, and my handle time overall was not negatively impacted. My handle time was among the best of my team!

Here's how this principle applies to you. Whether you are dealing with a customer or working through an internal process, it does not matter. When you need to pass along a project, a message, or something of importance to a coworker, customer, or a colleague, as often as possible, do a warm transfer in person. If that's not possible, do it by phone.

Two reasons for this: you're ensuring that the message gets to the intended recipient. We are all bombarded through our inboxes. What if they missed the email? What if they meant to follow up on it, got busy, and never got back to it?

Another benefit of following through by phone or in person is that it strengthens working relationships. It does take a little bit longer, but the communication is guaranteed to be more effective by phone or in person than via text or email. Stronger morale and more effective communication – Win/Win!

Applying these tools will help you positively impact and influence the people who work with you, your customers, and vendors. It especially works well to use empathy in your personal life. Whether it comes naturally to you, and especially if it **does not** come naturally to you, learning how to empathize with the people around you is an invaluable personal and professional skill.

Unleash your superpower of empathy and watch your impact and influence grow!

Empathy – Placing Myself in Others' Shoes
My Next Best Steps

_____

_____

_____

Chapter 4

Attitude

I'm sure you've heard the expression, "Our attitude is the one thing we can control in life." How we respond to situations, to other people, to opportunities, to setbacks, all of these responses are personal choices.

Our choices, over time, add up to our outlook in life and the direction we are headed.

When you encounter people, situations, challenges, or opportunities, do you respond to them, or do you react? A response is thoughtful, patient, measured, and wise, while a reaction is emotionally driven, hasty, often leading to regret.

How do you see your life? Is every day full of one interesting choice after another or just chance experiences?

Do you view life rationally, reasonably, with purpose, or do you see life happening to you randomly?

By honestly answering these questions, it can help reveal how you perceive life. A common attribute of Leaders, regardless of their age, experience, or role, is that they tend to respond, make choices, and believe that life is working ***for them***, not happening to them.

A positive attitude is infectious. So is a negative one! We know that bad news travels faster and likes to be shared far more than the good news. That means that it requires a greater amount of positivity to affect a team, an organization, a company, or a group of people.

Are you up to the task? Do you have a sense of ownership of your own life choices and how you can positively impact others? You may be much more of a Leader than you realize.

Thinking

There's a verse in the Bible that says, "As a man thinks in his heart, so is he." Interesting how thinking is connected to the heart, commonly understood as the seat of our emotions. What do our thoughts have to do with our attitude?

A great deal! If your mind is as active as mine is, you're constantly thinking. It's rare for my mind NOT to be chewing on something, NOT to be thinking about opportunities, conversations, or next best steps.

But what are we thinking? What do we keep in our minds? You may have heard of the book, *The Power of Positive Thinking*, by Norman Vincent Peale. That book has sold millions of copies worldwide over the decades.

So why does it seem like there's not an abundance of positively thinking people in the world?

There are a couple reasons for this. We are bombarded every day by troubling messages through various media outlets: the news, online, social media, conversations, and more. On top of that, we have our own thoughts about ourselves and our lives that are also rolling around in our heads. The amount of messages that we receive on a daily basis is overwhelming.

That's the challenge of being in a high technology society. We are constantly ingesting information. While we may not consciously think on these things, our subconscious mind absolutely is. And that's why it's so important that we consciously sort through our thoughts. Just like you clean out your basement - keeping this, not sure about that, pitching that for sure!, why do we even have this anymore?

Before we can impact and influence others, we have to be diligent about addressing our own thoughts. We need to proactively feed our minds with the messages that will help us succeed in life, that are positive, that are growth-focused, that are abundance-minded, that look at the opportunities versus the problems.

I truly hope that when you are done reading this book, your mind will be filled with encouraging truths as you pursue your Heroic Leadership.

Optimism

Did you know the word optimism shares the same root as optometry? That's right! Optimism has the same root word as the medical profession that takes care of peoples' sight. Optimism, then, is not a feeling or an attitude. It's what we see.

How often do we let things in life distract, obscure, hide, or bury our BHAGs, our dreams, our desire to make a difference in the world?

Has life gotten hazy for you? Does it seem out of focus for you?

We go to the optometrist when our eyesight isn't what it should be. Why? It's a combination of reasons: safety, health, and working ability. It's the same way with optimism.

How we view life affects our health, and our level of achievement. Take a moment to honestly assess how you're seeing life. If it's lacking in clarity, ask for insight from people you trust. If you're feeling troubled, get encouragement from people who believe in you, your potential, your character, and your determination.

Going to trusted sources of encouragement, counsel, and insight will help strengthen your optimism, how you see the world. Make sure you're doing this regularly. Most of the extraordinarily successful people I know have trusted counselors, advisors, mentors, and coaches in their lives. It's one of the reasons for their success.

Outlook on life

One company car I had during a sales role was quite distinctive. It was a bright blue, shiny, Dodge Dart. What was intriguing to me, was that when I started driving that car, all of a sudden, I noticed a lot more Dodge Darts on the road. Did other people, all of a sudden, decide to drive the same kind of car that I had?

No. I just started noticing more of them because I was sitting behind the wheel of a Dodge Dart. My outlook on life changed based on where I was sitting, based on my viewpoint, based on my experience.

What's your outlook on life? It could be far more difficult to have a positive outlook on life if your surroundings are not positive or are challenging. But you can change that. Not your surroundings or even your circumstances, but your outlook.

Think of it this way.... Our outlook on life is like the frame of a picture. A shabby, paint peeling, ugly frame around a beautiful piece of art automatically detracts from the value of the piece. But a golden, detailed, elegant frame elevates the value of any piece of art, no matter how simple.

How you frame your life has a tremendous impact on what you experience in life.

One way that I frame my day is to start my day with gratitude. When I pull out of the driveway, I share three things, at least, that I'm grateful for from the day before. They have to be new ones; I can't recycle any of them. They have to be fresh from the day before. I can have more than three, but I need to have at least three new ones from the day before.

This frames my day with gratefulness, and it helps me be more aware of things in my life for which I am grateful. When we start our day with gratitude, knowing we are going to be thankful tomorrow for the good things that happened for us today, we begin to train our attention to look out for those good things coming our way.

How are you framing your life? If you see your potential as that shabby, paint peeling, unattractive border, it automatically takes value away from your potential Leadership.

But, if we see that our character, our determination, our desire for excellence, and our commitment to help others succeed is framing our opportunities, then more and better opportunities will come our way.

Be careful how you frame your day. It's powerful!

Perspective

What did you learn?

The way we grow, mature, and progress personally and professionally comes through a powerful life tool called perspective.

When I deployed to Iraq in 2010 with the Ohio Army National Guard, our unit was composed of well over 100 soldiers. When we stepped off the plane into Iraq, I was immediately struck by the poverty and destruction of a war-ravaged, impoverished country. It was in stark contrast to even some of the poorest areas back in the United States.

On top of these living conditions all around us, we were faced with the incredible responsibility of lives being entrusted to our care. Our unit provided warning for rocket and mortar attacks on U.S. bases throughout Iraq. It was our job to make sure that if a round was fired at any military installation, we would sound a localized alarm for people to get under cover before the rounds struck.

I learned how to work efficiently under stress, I learned the value of strong teamwork, I discovered what I was capable of achieving, and most importantly, I came away with perspective. Perspective on what a good day or a bad day looked like when lives depended on us. I learned how much I had to be grateful for back at home in comparison to how people lived in Iraq.

The sad part of this experience was that some of the soldiers who deployed in our unit returned back to the United States at the same level of maturity and perspective as when they left. They didn't gain from the experience.

Perspective is opportunity, it's not a guarantee.

It's available to all of us to learn and grow from challenging times. But the ones who are intentional about learning from what went well and what did not go well, are the ones who are the most effective Leaders.

If you're not learning from life, you're not going to be an effective leader. If you're not learning from life, you're not standing still, you're regressing. You're falling behind.

Those who aspire to be Heroic Leaders do not give themselves the luxury of being comfortable in life, settling for good enough, or not learning from life experiences. Because you choose to learn from your life experiences, you have the ability to bring Heroic Impact to others' lives.

Take a quick snapshot of yourself. Look at where you are today, then think back to where you were just a few years ago. Have you learned? Have you improved? Have you gained perspective? Is the quality of your work higher than before? Have you impacted people positively?

It's good to reflect on where we came from, where we are currently, and where we want to go. Heroic Leaders embrace the fact that our lives can always be better. It's not discouraging to us; it's inspiring.

Confidence

Another aspect of positivity is confidence. "I'm confident that we will find a solution to the problem." "I'm confident that you can achieve your goals." "I'm confident that my good choices over time will add up to better and better opportunities."

What's really cool about confidence is that you can borrow it from others that you trust. In 2019, I added a business mentor to my life. You wouldn't know it by looking at him, but Ken is a six-time world record holder for powerlifting. I was impressed by his profile, and the quality of the people who recommended I have coffee with him. We hit it off so well that our first conversation lasted for four hours!

I am so grateful that I took that step of adding a respected, accomplished business mentor to my life. Ken added value to me by identifying my potential, my qualities, and my opportunities. He added best practices, business insights, and goal achievement strategies. All of these were significant in building my personal brand. Ken's positive impact on my life has led to one fantastic opportunity after another, as a public speaker, as a business coach, as a consultant, as a facilitator, and as an author.

I borrowed Ken's confidence. In 2019, I had no idea where I would be by 2024, but here I am writing this book on Leadership. I didn't know that I would have spoken to thousands of people in person and many thousands of people online. But Ken saw that potential in me, encouraging and equipping me to grow in my potential.

That's what Leaders do.

And I've had the privilege to pour that confidence into others' lives now. Ken's positive impact in my life didn't just stay with me; it spread to others.

That's the potential that we all have, those of us who desire to impact and influence others. You don't need a certain age, a certain title, a certain number of followers, or to be well known in order to be a Heroic Leader. You simply have to find people who need encouragement and some ideas on how to achieve their goals. By sharing ideas with them on how to do that, you ARE being a Leader. And if you're helping them aspire to excellence and a goal far bigger than themselves, you are a Heroic Leader.

Solutions

Anybody, and I mean anybody, can spot the problem. But fewer people also suggest solutions to that problem. I've had the privilege of speaking with a number of business owners, senior executives, and corporate Leaders. They all appreciate people who approach them with concerns **and** ideas to address those concerns.

Do you spot the potential solutions to the challenges in your company, in your life, in others' lives? If you do, that's a strong trait of Leadership. It's easy, almost effortless, to point out problems, what's not going right. It takes creativity, initiative, and concern for others to notice the issues and generate ideas that could help.

Best of all, if you're a solutions-focused Leader, and you're intentional about impacting others, you'll begin to attract others who share the same values. It's not that hard to be different from most. One of the best ways is to share solutions that accompany a challenge.

Energy giver

Picture a car battery in your mind. There are people in your life who add energy to your battery. They're like a battery charger. They help your energy levels go up.

Then there are a great deal of people who don't take energy away from you, but they don't charge your battery either. They're neutral in their impact.

Then, there are people who drain your energy. This isn't always malicious. Some people are simply unaware of the value of your time, of the goals you desire to achieve, of the things that are most important to you, of how the words they say and the actions they take can negatively impact others. Yes, there are people who do this intentionally, but I find that to be rare. A sizable number of people are unaware how their negativity, lack of self-awareness, and word choices take energy away from others.

How about you? Before you think that this is a personality concern, being an energy giver has nothing to do with your personality. You don't have to be the class clown, the person who's always smiling, always bubbly, always joyful.

You can give energy by being quiet and actively listening to someone. You can give energy by genuinely caring for them. You can give energy by giving to others without expecting anything in return. You can give energy by asking well-worded questions and listening for the answers. There are so many ways we can give energy to others.

Life has a way of taking enough energy from us. That's why Heroic Leaders have an opportunity to significantly impact all those around them. Because they give energy. Because they care about others more than themselves. Yes, you have goals and dreams you're pursuing, but you want to do that ***with*** others. You want others to Win, too. You want others to experience tremendous success.

As a Leader, it's important for you to identify who in your life is an energy giver, and who in your life is an energy taker. While you may not be able to eliminate the energy takers, find ways to limit your interaction with them.

Jim Rohn famously said that we are the average of the 5 people we spend the most time with. Choose wisely as to who you intentionally spend your free time with. You will not be able to completely separate yourself from energy takers. But you can limit it. I highly recommend it.

Attitude – What I CAN Control

My Next Best Steps

_____

_____

_____

Chapter 5

Do

"It's not what we say, it's what we do." I heard this phrase often growing up, and it's still true today. Our actions do speak louder than our words. They reveal to us and others what we believe and whether others can depend on us.

What we do is incredibly important, especially if we desire to be Heroic Leaders. So how do we have a life filled with effective action taking? Where does it start? How do we do more of it?

As we mentioned in the previous chapter, our thinking has a tremendous impact on our choices in life. The thoughts that we keep in our mind, the thoughts that we feed intentionally to our mind, and the thoughts that we get rid of directly influence the actions we take.

But there's something even stronger than our thoughts that directly affects our actions-- our beliefs.

The actions I take every day reveal what I genuinely believe. Sometimes, this aligns with what I'm thinking and saying. Other times, they don't match up. I might say one thing, but my actions reveal another.

Do you believe that you're a Leader? Do you believe that you're a Heroic Leader? Your actions reveal if you believe you're a Leader or not.

In 2021, I made a personal commitment to read and notate one book per week. I was in a consulting role, and I wanted to be a resource for the companies I would be meeting with. I resolved to study some of the best thought leaders and their books on topics like Leadership, growth, sales, service, influence, change, teamwork, finances, and time management. Not only did I learn a great deal in those two years, I developed quite a reading list. I still have all those handwritten notes.

It was one thing to say that I wanted to read and notate over 100 books in two years. It was a whole other thing to achieve it.

One book I read was written by John Cotter entitled, *A True Sense of Urgency*. Cotter identifies three broad categories for urgency personally and professionally.

The first kind is no sense of urgency, or apathy in a person or an organization. They just don't care. Easy to spot.

But it was the second category, that was more challenging to identify. This was a false sense of urgency. People and organizations like this are extremely busy, but only somewhat productive. Cotter said that busyness can mask the lack of effective work. I'm sure people are coming to your mind right now who are always busy, always stressed, always having too much to do.

It becomes far clearer to me now to identify people with a true sense of urgency – self-motivated people who want to Win, Today. They ask one key question: "What do I need to do Today to progress towards my goals?" Professionals with a true sense of urgency know how to execute very well.

An ability to execute is one of the most essential qualities I look for in new relationships (personally and professionally), in potential collaborations, and especially in potential clients.

Action

Remember that short, wrinkled, green guy with big ears, who famously said: "Do or do not. There is no try?" You know the guy I'm talking about! Taking decisive action is another admirable trait of Leaders.

A good friend of mine has been involved in community theater for many years. It's interesting that before the director shouts, "Action!," there are two steps before that. "Lights" --illumination, insight, vision, clarity. Before you can take decisive action, you need to have these things in place first. But the second direction is, "Camera!" What does that have to do with our lives?

Before the show could start, they needed to make sure that what is about to occur is captured. If we just go through life from one experience to another, but aren't observing, assessing, evaluating, or improving on those experiences and choices, then we're simply wandering through life, missing out on the impact or influence we want to have in others' lives. Lights, camera, then action! We can act more decisively when we can see and when we are prepared to learn from what we experience.

Character

I studied this word recently. Fascinating! Character comes from the old Greek that had to do with embossing leather or engraving pottery. It was leaving your mark on something. Like a trademark. If you're doing quality work and putting others as more important than yourself, you are leaving your mark; you are displaying your character for your team, for your company, for your community.

One of the encouraging things about character is that you can improve it --it can be changed for the better and leave a lasting impression on others. You can achieve this, regardless of your age, role, experience, or abilities. Leaving your mark requires intentional pursuit of excellence; leaving a good impression requires this, too. I look back on my life, and I see many times where I did not make good choices. The impressions I left on others was not positive. I did not lead effectively in those times, because my character, my trademark, what I was known for, was not positive.

When I took ownership of my life and my choices, I began to make better choices, to fill my mind with better thoughts, to aspire to greater goals in life, to pursue excellence, and to value others' success as more important than my own. Then my character changed. The impression I had on others changed, too. The ability to impact and influence others changed for the good.

So can yours. Even if you're on the right track, as you grow, mature, learn, and pour into others, your character will change, too.

Think of it this way, if character is leaving your mark, then the bigger impact and influence you have means that you're leaving a bigger and bigger mark in life. Our mark could be a microscopic engraving on a shot glass, or, it could be the letter "H" in the Hollywood sign. Our character is not limited by our age, our experiences, or our role. Our character can be as large as we desire, if we intentionally pursue the right things, with the right people, and the right opportunities.

Integrity

I know, I know. I'm a word nerd. If you didn't already know it, I love to study the meanings and the origins of words. I also did this for integrity. Integrity means wholeness. Are you used to thinking that integrity means doing the right thing when no one's around? That's an aspect of it. But what does it mean to be a whole person?

It means that we're complete. People aren't getting pieces of us. People aren't getting one experience at one place and then another experience in another place. We're the same, regardless of our circumstances, the people around us, the challenges we face, or the opportunities we pursue.

That wasn't true of me for a good part of my life. I relied too heavily on what others thought about me, what others said about me. I borrowed their perception. I tried to be the person that those people would like. I was a chameleon. I tried to adapt to whatever I thought would help people like me. Others' approval drove my decision making. By myself, I often did what I wanted, not considering others. But around other people, it was important to me to look good, to earn their favor, to be liked. I was not a whole person.

I look back at those years and see the poor decisions that I made, the lack of impact that I had on others. It's different to be liked rather than to have impact in people's lives. It's different to be impressive than it is to make a lasting impression.

What's the difference?

One of the factors that makes it different is my motivation. When I was younger, looking good, others' approval, that was most important to me. Now that I'm a whole person, it's more about doing my absolute best and helping others do the same. Whether you see me on the stage during a keynote speech, whether you encounter me facilitating a workshop, whether you read this book or watch my videos, when you meet me in person, I'm the same guy.

I have integrity now.

It can be more of a challenge to be a complete person when you're younger. But I firmly believe that if you're surrounded with the right people who help you with maturity, wisdom, self-awareness, and pursuing meaningful goals and priorities, you can experience being whole, too.

It's the only way that we can have Win/Win impact and influence others' lives. There are plenty of people out there impacting and influencing others' lives, but they're not the same person everywhere they go. They don't have integrity.

You can. And the world needs that desperately.

Goalsetting and Goal Getting

I told you that my business mentor, Ken, helped me achieve goals with proven strategies. I highly recommend you get a copy of his book, *Don't Fake The Funk*.

Also known as Mr. Biz, Ken is an accomplished consultant, radio show host, author, and thought leader. When I utilized his proven approach to accomplish the BHAG's in my life, I began to see considerable progress towards those goals.

Setting goals is good. Writing down your goals is even better. Writing down highly specific goals is excellent, but the most important part about goals is getting them done, is accomplishing them. I know that's easier said than done, but here are some tips on how to get your goals done.

If you're going to set goals, make them highly specific, measurable, and build in a couple of critical habits so that you're far more likely to achieve them.

Number one – write them down. A University of Kansas study showed that written goals are 30% more likely to be achieved than just goals that we set in our minds. Why? Because everything our eyes see, our subconscious mind is processing. Write down your goals and keep them in front of you – be what you see. Our subconscious is constantly working on those goals to help us achieve them.

Number two – add accountability. I do not mean people who will make you do what you don't want to do. That's not accountability; that's babysitting.

Every week, I send a summary of my activities towards my BHAGs to a small group of individuals. Occasionally, these people comment or recommend stepping up activity in certain areas. Often, they don't respond. That's fine. The reason I send the email is not for them to respond. The reason I send the email is to hold myself accountable to my goals.

That's the key difference of true accountability versus the buzzword I hear often. True accountability is actually self-accountability.

I am most effective when I'm holding myself accountable to my own goals.

My group email is not so they will check up on me; it's me checking up on myself. It's making sure I am doing the activities I need to do to achieve my BHAGs.

Do you have people in your life like that? It could be one person, it could be ten. It's best if it's more than one person. But even if it's only one person, they can be all the additional accountability you need to make sure that you're staying on top of your goal pursuits.

One caution: in order for this to work effectively, you have to be honest. If you didn't do the work, you can't say you did.

Highly successful people do not lie to themselves.

If you want to achieve your BHAG's, write down your highly specific goals, hold yourself accountable to the activities to achieve those goals, and be honest with yourself.

Over time, the results will be evident. Consistent action towards highly specific goals results in measurable progress that you and others in your life can clearly see.

Take your next best step.

Too many people know what their next best step is, but they overthink it, they're slow to act, they're concerned about the risk, they're unsure if it will work. I understand all those concerns. But I have heard a sizable number of extraordinarily successful people say you just need to start.

If you know the next best step, take it. Of course, things will change after you make that decision. The plan you have in mind is probably not the one you'll finish with. It will likely take longer, perhaps far longer, than you thought. All of those things happen frequently.

But Leaders don't allow those bumps in the road to deter them from continuing to pursue their goals. They continue to take the next best step.

Think of it this way. If a Big Hairy Audacious Goal takes 1,000 steps from the time you start to the time you accomplish it, then it would be better to start earlier than later, wouldn't it? True, we don't know exactly how many steps, how many actions, it will take to achieve our BHAGs. But we do know for certain that it will take the first one, and then the one after that, and then the one after that to get closer to achieving those goals.

Have you asked people you respect, "Does this seem like a promising idea? Here's what I'm thinking, what are your thoughts?" If those people, who have no skin in the game -

-they do not benefit financially from your success or lose money if your idea doesn't work--they are simply speaking to the idea itself. And if they tell you that's a promising idea, take your next best step. And the one after that. And the one after that. Check in with those counselors from time to time, just to make sure you're on the right track.

Leaders take action. They pursue their goals. And even if it takes an exceptionally long time to achieve their BHAGs, they accomplish a substantial number of smaller goals along the way. That's why they're called Big Hairy Audacious Goals. They take a great amount of time, effort, and grit to achieve. If everybody achieved Big Hairy Audacious Goals, they wouldn't be big, hairy, or audacious, would they?!

Write down your highly specific goals, keep them in front of you, and then get after them.

Walking the Talk

This is the last aspect of taking action as a Leader. Everyone could do this; everyone should do this. It's far more effective with coworkers when a Heroic Leader like you chooses to take decisive, quality actions. Especially when those around you are lukewarm or not interested, this will differentiate you significantly. And even if your current company is not a good fit, your future opportunity will appreciate the Heroic Leadership qualities you bring with you to your new role.

I had the privilege of working with an excellent Leader in retail. Tim modeled what he expected of his staff. Our company provided uniforms, shoes, luggage, and other accessories for airline employees in the Northern Kentucky Cincinnati Airport. Only airline employees had access to the store, so these retail stores were not open to the general public. A sizable number of our customers were professionals: pilots, flight attendants, and more. Looking professional in their uniforms was quite important to them. In the store, we needed to reflect that kind of brand.

Tim not only took immense pride in how the store looked, but he jumped right in along with us to do one of the most hated tasks: stocking inventory. When the truck would back up to the door, Tim would be right in there with us, helping move the boxes and unload what was inside. The contents could be uniforms, could be shoes, could be pilot hats, could be trinkets and toys with airline logos on them. Tim always had other responsibilities as the store manager – meetings, reports, hiring, training – but he always made time to work alongside us. He walked the talk. He modeled what a Heroic Leader should do. He could've told us what to do, and our crew would've done it. But it had far greater impact and influence for him to do it along with us.

That's the essence of being a Leader --to bring others along as someone who's been there before, as a guide, as someone doing it with us, not telling us how to do it. Tim exemplified what being a Leader looks like, and he was a good man to work for. He was patient, he was kind, he was understanding, he had excellent customer service. The customer service that he displayed and trained all of us in, was so good that some pilots or flight attendants would wait to buy the same item from our smaller store that was harder to get to than the other locations that were larger and had easier access. Our customer experience was that much better.

That's the practical side of Heroic Leadership. It's absolutely profitable. It retains clients and team members. It differentiates from other businesses in the same industry. It makes a difference in the lives of the ones who experience it.

Regardless of your age, your experience, your education, your role, or your abilities, if you take decisive action with excellence, and with others' best interest at heart, you ARE a Heroic Leader.

Take that next best step. Achieve your specific, written goals. Make a difference in the lives of those around you.

Do – Taking Decisive Action

My Next Best Steps

———————————————————

———————————————————

———————————————————

Chapter 6
Earn Trust

Before the pandemic, ZenDesk conducted a global survey. They wanted to know what qualities were most important to consumers, what guided their buying decisions. Tens of thousands of respondents from over 100 countries revealed an interesting shift in priorities.

Rather than choosing lowest price or brand recognition, customers were valuing 3 qualities: speed, convenience, and know, like, and trust. The first two responses are measurable and completely understandable – sooner and easier. But how can consumers know, like, and trust the company they do business with?

The same way they know, like, and trust Leaders. Do they follow through on their promises? How do they treat their team members and their customers? Is there social proof that they live out their values?

Trust is the most valued social currency in the workplace, the marketplace, and within interpersonal relationships. I always had a hunch this was true. But in the fall of 2021, my hunch was confirmed.

As an exhibitor at a healthcare conference in San Diego, I had the privilege of hearing David Horsager speak. David is the founder of The Trust Institute. His compelling presentation underlined the importance of earning and keeping trust. I highly recommend David's content as an invaluable source of actionable, data-rich approaches to earning and keeping trust within your business.

Trust is like a bank account. When we earn others' trust, it's like we're making a deposit into our trust account with them. When something doesn't go according to plan, a withdrawal is made from our trust account.

The ultimate goal is to make so many trust deposits into our account with other people that the occasional misstep is barely noticed. This is especially important for those of us who desire to be Heroic Leaders.

Our seemingly insignificant actions with others, either directly with them or with others that they observe, make deposits into our trust account with them. That's why everything we do contributes to, or takes away, trust.

That's also why anyone can be a Heroic Leader, positively impacting others, if they focus on consistently giving value to others.

The people who want followers, fans, and fame don't care about keeping trust. They want to earn just enough trust to convince their fans and followers to buy from them or do what they say. They're often charming, persuasive, and charismatic, almost magnetic to others.

My good friend, David Meltzer, shared with me that Tony Robbins said the golden ticket for sales used to be NLP – Neuro Linguistic Programming. Tony said it's changed, though. It's now Authenticity.

That's the problem for charismatic people. They lack authenticity. When their followers begin to interact with them, they discover a disconnect between their expectations and the charmer's lack of genuineness. And they fall away, disillusioned.

Charisma attracts, but authenticity retains.

Charm is like a magnet that's strong enough to attach to a metal object, but too weak to remain connected with any kind of movement.

Authenticity, on the other hand, is like a powerful magnet that draws in others so strongly, that when there's any kind of movement (changes or challenges), the magnet and metal object stay firmly connected.

This is why anyone can be a Heroic Leader if they will genuinely work to earn and keep the trust of those around them.

Trust Fall

Have you ever worked at a summer camp? For one summer, I was the counselor for 10-year-old boys. Whew! Did I develop an appreciation for my parents that summer!

The ranchers would arrive on Sunday. The first activity on Monday was The Challenge Course, a low-element ropes course where no harnesses were needed for safety. The events were still quite challenging, though. Every cabin was required to complete The Trust Fall.

For those of you who may not have experienced a trust fall, let me explain what that is. One person stands on a taller object, in this case, they were consecutively taller logs standing on end. The person completing the trust fall would stand on the tallest log end with their back to two lines of people facing each other, arms outstretched. The event required the person on the tall log to trust the people behind them, falling backwards into their arms. This requires a great amount of trust by the person falling backwards.

Not all 10-year-old boys are built the same. Most were about the same size. But every once in a while, we would get a larger-than-average boy up on the log. It takes even greater trust for that larger child to believe that his new bunkmates are going to catch him.

Some of these children came from tough backgrounds. I made a personal commitment to never drop a single boy. It didn't matter if the other 9 ranchers ran for their lives, I would make sure that child was caught.

These children had been dropped, figuratively, many times in their lives. I didn't want to be added to their list of people they couldn't trust. We only had a week together; I wanted our time to be a positive, encouraging experience. I'm grateful to say that in all 8 of those bunkhouses, we never dropped a single boy.

There are two insights to this experience I need to point out to you.

Some of the best advice I received from the camp director was how to prepare the person about to complete the trust fall. They instructed them to stretch out their arms, palms facing away from each other, then cross their arms at the wrist and bring their gripped hands back underneath their arms, clasping them to their chest.

What's your natural reaction when falling backwards? That's right....our arms want to fling out. You can imagine how bad this would be if the falling person flung their arms out as they fell, whacking the faces of the people trying to catch them!

By preparing the person about to fall, we prevented the catchers from getting hurt and greatly increased the odds that the falling person would be caught. Win/Win!

In our lives, even when we extend trust to others, sometimes we're going to get whacked by them. Even with good intentions, this happens often. Why?

Those people weren't prepared to trust you; they were going off of past experiences. They had been figuratively dropped by others, many times.

You can be a Heroic Leader to others simply by being one of the few people they can count on, one of the few that will catch them, no matter what. One of the few they can trust.

Sales Success

Repeatedly in my career, I earned record sales in industries with no previous experience. Not because I'm a born salesperson, not because I can "sell you this pen." But because I have the ability to earn trust. How did I achieve that in a sales setting?

I put myself in their shoes. I learned their world. I asked lots of well-worded questions to understand what a good day looked like, what a tough day looked like. Then I determined if I had solutions that could help them do their job better, safer, more effectively, with higher quality. My goal was not to sell them the most expensive thing I had. I found out what their greatest need was and saw if I had a solution to address it.

I learned how to ask genuinely, "How can I help you?" Sometimes, the answer wasn't obvious. Other times, what I perceived as being a greater priority, wasn't most important to them.

The questions we ask, both the quality of them and the genuine care behind them, can enable any of us to be Heroic Leaders.

Under Promise, Over Deliver

Another excellent way to earn and keep trust with others is to build margin into your promises. Here's what I mean....

When I was in sales, and a customer needed a proposal, I would ask them if delivering the quote by the end of business Friday would work for them. Their answer was often "Yes." But I knew that I could deliver the proposal by end of business Thursday.

So why would I offer Friday? Because life happens. Do your weeks every go perfectly according to your plans? Nope, hardly ever!

Whenever possible, I would make sure I gave myself extra time to deliver the quote earlier than promised. This built strong trust quickly because of their experiences with other salespeople. To make a sale, salespeople sometimes promise things they can't deliver by the time they say they can follow through.

By adding a little extra time to my estimate, I gained more trust, rather than someone promising a ridiculously fast response time with no follow through.

Now, if Friday morning came around, and I was not sure I could deliver the quote on time, I would reach out to the customer, stating that delays came up for me this past week. I would then ask if Monday end of business would work for them. If yes, I would make sure it arrived first thing Monday morning.

If not, I would get help or work extra hours to make sure the customer had what they needed on time.

If you follow through with what you say you'll do, you will earn and keep trust, regardless of your age, experience, role, or degrees. That will automatically place you as a Leader in the mind of those you're positively impacting.

Overbearing

Do you know where the word "trust" comes from? It's Scandinavian in origin, and it's where we get our word "truss." That's right! The boards that support your roof.

How fascinating that a key element in a safe, strong home connects with trust. Two Leadership principles here....

First, there need to be enough trusses in place for the roof to hold up. A cheap roof has too few trusses, resulting in sagging roof boards between each truss. This takes years to become evident. And if that home receives an unexpected amount of snowfall, the roof can collapse or break in spots.

In the same way, if we do not have enough support for others, it becomes apparent over time and can even end the relationship when unexpected challenges arise.

Secondly, the other extreme is putting in too many trusses. How could too much support be a bad thing?! It's more expensive, unnecessary, and adds additional weight to the top of the house. Now the support for the roof becomes overbearing, too much.

When leaders become intrusive, demanding, and micromanaging, that's the same as including too many trusses. It's unwelcome, unnecessary, and creates extra work.

As aspiring Heroic Leaders, we need to have enough support to get through challenging times, but not so much that our colleagues feel controlled or overwhelmed.

How do we know how many trusses are enough? Just like there's a building code that tells home builders how many trusses are enough, experienced mentors and trusted Leaders can tell you how much support, guidance, and interaction is appropriate.

This is also why inexperienced leaders, like I was!, can overstep their bounds unknowingly. While it comes from good intentions, the way it feels to others is not positive and takes away trust and influence.

Find an authentic, experienced Leader you respect, and ask them for their wisdom on Leading others.

Responsive

One business owner I worked for had a saying that stuck with me: "Silence is deadly." In sales especially, when customers do not hear from us for a while, they usually assume the worst – we're not interested in them, we're too busy to stay in touch, we have more important things to do. It's especially important when the customer is expecting a proposal or an update. Sometimes, the salespeople who respond the quickest, get the work, even if they were not the favorite option.

How does being responsive connect with Heroic Leadership? It earns trust. If those around us can count on responsive, accurate communication, we will differentiate ourselves from what they typically experience.

When I was new to B2B sales, I was shocked how often I heard from prospective clients that they never heard back from other companies. To me, this was missing out from a ridiculously simple habit: get the customer what they need as soon as you can.

Several business owners I know also say that they win a significant amount of business simply because their competitors don't respond.

Why would someone in sales not follow through? Why would leaders not be responsive? The answer is the same for both questions....

Because it's not important enough to them. I know that sounds harsh, but it's true. We always do what is most important to us, no matter what we might ***say*** is important.

Again, this is a key area where you can distinguish yourself as a Heroic Leader because responsiveness is still not typical in the workplace, in the marketplace, or through interpersonal relationships.

Truth Tellers

Jim Collins coined a fascinating concept he calls, "The Genius of And." Rather than certain concepts being only one or the other, he recommends considering if both ideas can co-exist.

- Can someone be honest AND tactful?
- Can someone rely on facts AND feelings to communicate with others?
- Can someone focus on achieving their Big Hairy Audacious Goals AND their progress?
- Can a business focus on 5-star Service AND Profitability?

Yes, they can.

Applying "The Genius of And" means that we can be tactful truth tellers when influencing others. Extremes are always dangerous when working to positively influence others. We should avoid "I call it like I see it" – truth that is too direct, causing unnecessary negative emotions. We also should not avoid telling the truth simply because it may be hard to hear. Timing is everything on this.

Simon Sinek had a video on social media that I greatly appreciated, addressing how to be tactfully truthful. He said that we must be aware of the emotions in the moment as to how directly truthful we can be.

For example, he shared a story where he attended a friend's play. The event was so poorly done that he would have left, had it not been for his friendship.

After the show was over, his excited friend asked him, "What did you think?"

Seeing that she was experiencing the thrill of acting out her own play, Simon stated that we was so grateful to see his friend in her own play, enjoying her passion. A day or two later, when the euphoric emotions had settled, he gently shared with her his observations.

We will earn and keep more trust if we are gentle truth tellers rather than popular cheerleaders or abrupt critics.

NOT According to Plan

One of the most effective ways to earn and keep trust may surprise you – when we make mistakes. Doesn't sound right, does it?

Any reasonable customer knows that we will never have perfect transactions every time. It's just not possible. Even horribly managed companies can handle a smooth transaction with no issues.

But the quality of our Leadership is best proven when things DO NOT go according to plan. That's when the people around us discover if we genuinely care about them and about giving our absolute best. If we do, we will work hard to make things right.

We expect mistakes to happen. We trust Leaders who own up to those mistakes, with no excuses, and deliver an experience that matches their own standards of excellence. While it may be tempting to pass along the blame (especially if it's partly others' fault), Heroic Leaders work to find the solution, not the blame. Does that describe you?

When I was an insecure, self-focused leader, it was most important for me to look good. When I chose to become a Heroic Leader, it was important to me for others to succeed, to have the best chance to succeed.

The former Navy S.E.A.L., Jocko Willink, in his book, *Extreme Ownership,* said that when the mission was a success, his team got the credit. When the mission was a failure, Leadership took responsibility.

Well said. THAT'S Heroic Leadership in action when things don't go according to plan.

Anyone can Lead like this. It's simply a choice to put others first. As simple as that sounds, it's not easy. And that's why Heroic Leadership is so rare.

Let's be the Leaders who give the credit and take the responsibility. We will earn and keep trust from people who value authentic Leaders, regardless of their age, experience, role, background, education, or personality.

Let's be trustworthy Heroic Leaders!

Trust – Earning and Keeping It

My Next Best Steps

_____

_____

_____

Chapter 7

Responsibility

It's a word that we've heard many, many times. I always understood it as a personal character trait that meant someone could be trusted. They were responsible.

When I studied the word, it surprised me. It literally means "able to respond." It's a neutral word. Able to respond doesn't indicate whether the outcome is positive, negative, or neutral. Just that someone is able to respond.

There's a difference between response and reaction. Responses are measured, thoughtful, wise. Reactions can be emotional, unstable, unpredictable, and late.

Being able to respond is an excellent quality. Often times, people do not respond at all, either from freezing in the situation, from the situation, or continually putting it off. Or they respond in a way that is for their own good only. It's measured, but it's not win-win.

A Heroic Leader is not only responsive in a timely manner, but in a way that's reasonable and includes others' best interest as well as their own - win-win.

Here are some attributes of being a responsible, Heroic Leader.

Honda Civic

In the last chapter, I mentioned my well-worn Honda Civic. I bought the car with just over 100,000 miles on it. A five-speed manual transmission, four-door, silver sedan, the car ran very well for many years. I owned the car for 11 years and put 230,000 miles on it. Same clutch and engine. Routine maintenance only, the car was hardly ever in the shop.

Reliability is one aspect of being responsible. When I turned the key in the ignition of my Civic, I was supremely confident it would get me from point A to point B. As I also mentioned in the previous chapter, I had 2 newer company cars that were in the shop more often than my Civic. There were times when I could not rely on those vehicles that I needed to get me to my sales appointments. Quite frustrating.

I did mention that my Honda Civic was well worn, didn't I? The paint job was peeling, the fenders were dented, and the underskirt was missing. But I could rely on that car.

Hollywood has done a fantastic job of crafting a misleading picture of heroic leaders, that look like Captain America or Wonder Woman. But that's not what Heroic Leadership looks like. A Heroic Leader can never be determined by their appearance. Since we cannot judge a book by its cover, we must apply the same measure objectively to ourselves. So what if we do not look "the part?" That's not the point. The point is: can others rely on you? That matters far more to them and to the overall success of your company than your appearance.

Ownership

Some confuse the quality of ownership as people who desire to control. Not at all! Ownership is treating every opportunity as if it was solely my responsibility. "If this was my company" - that kind of spirit. Whether I have ownership stake or not, do I treat the company and the opportunity as if it were my own?

Do you notice areas of improvement? Do you look for ways that your teammates are succeeding? Do you notice areas of friction that are impacting the customer experience? Do you have ideas on how your company could increase efficiency, profitability, and service?

You already possess the traits. Heroic Leaders treat every role, regardless of their role, as if it was their company.

My experience has been that taking initiative like this is sometimes welcomed, and sometimes not. It depends on the leadership and the culture. If one or both are dysfunctional, ownership can be perceived as taking control. In the right environment, however, it's a game changer.

Professional

Regardless of what you do, do you see yourself as a professional? The adjective "professional" used to be automatically applied to jobs in certain industries, confusing white-collar jobs or office work as the only professional roles. It's a very wrong assumption to make.

Professionalism is displayed in the quality of your work - always learning to improve your skills and abilities, being punctual (not just on time, barely, but always a few minutes early to expect the unexpected), and keeping up on the best practices of what to do, what not to do, and what's new in your industry.

Above all, very clearly pursuing a career path within the company. If the company culture is healthy, and the opportunities are sound, communicating intentionally to management that you desire to have opportunities for growth, for promotion, indicates that you see a future with the company. All those qualities contribute to being a professional in the workplace.

In what ways can Heroic Leaders equip themselves so they can respond appropriately in any situation, especially the challenging ones? Here are several ideas.

Active Listening

When I was an eager but unprepared, aspiring leader, I listened to respond. It was more important to me to be valued and respected, not to understand what the other person was saying. It revealed my insecurity as an immature leader.

When we listen to understand, the speaker feels valued. In addition to this, we have a better understanding and a clearer picture of where they're coming from. This not only encourages open communication, but it gives me more information to work with as a Leader. After all, how can we encourage, empower, or equip people if we don't have a clear understanding of where they're coming from?

Emotional Intelligence

Especially in challenging conversations, it can be exceedingly difficult to remain calm and composed. Here are a few things to consider when going into a potentially difficult conversation.

Remember to breathe. I know this seems strange, perhaps, but when we react to a tense situation, our breaths can become more shallow, more rapid, and lead to an increased heart rate. All of these add more tension to a sticky situation. Remember to breathe, pause before responding, and be mindful of your tone and body language. We communicate far more with our body language than we might realize. Our words are the least important, because ***how*** we say something is more important than ***what*** we say. Our tone, combined with our body language, can communicate the wrong message.

Another good thing to do is to prepare mentally and emotionally before a difficult conversation and work through the scenarios of how that person might react. This helps us to plan our response beforehand. If the conversation goes easier than expected, wonderful! If it's just as challenging, or more so, we still prepared ourselves emotionally to prevent as many unintended causes for increased tension.

Focus on the Solution

Fix the problem, not the blame. We talked about this earlier in the book about a positive attitude focusing on solutions. By reiterating the truth that we want to achieve a win-win solution, the other party realizes that we are not trying to find out who's to blame. We want to find a resolution.

Use well worded questions like "What can we do to move forward?" Or "What ideas do you have to address this?" If there's any part of what we might have said or communicated better, take ownership of that. I do not recommend taking ownership of something just to ease the tension. Heroic Leaders need to be tactful truth tellers. If you did not contribute to the issue in any way, don't take responsibility for something that you didn't do. That's not authentic.

Empathy

We covered this aspect of Heroic Leadership in great detail, so this will be a very brief thought. It's important that we combine an empathetic approach while maintaining agreed-upon standards. Compromise comes in the form of being open to a different point of view. But it should not involve lessening or lowering standards simply to smooth out demanding situations. Compromise on point of view or potential solutions, yes. Never compromise on values and standards.

Direct

This is something I am still working on improving. It was so important to me that my words not be offensive, that often they lacked clarity and directness. This created confusion and misunderstanding, leading to the need for unnecessary additional communication.

If people are repeatedly asking you to explain what you mean, you may need to focus on improving clarity and specificity in your communication.

Along with being clear in your language, our expectations should be clear as well. I know you may not be in a decision-making role. But communicating to your teammates and your supervisors what your expectations are for them and for yourself can avoid unnecessary friction, while giving them clearer understanding of what your intentions are.

Being clear and direct while being respectful is especially important in the challenging conversations. Our word choice, our body language, our tone, and our direct honesty all contribute to a respectful work environment. I have found that the greatest challenge is to be respectful towards someone whose choices and behavior do not typically earn others' respect, especially those that I report to. That's when it's most important to respect the position.

One show that I really enjoyed when I deployed to Iraq in 2010 was the series *Band of Brothers*. An immature, incompetent officer was replaced by a successful, Heroic Leader. As the unit was about to deploy, the successful Leader and immature leader encountered one another. Because of his successful Leadership capabilities, the Heroic Leader now outranked the incompetent leader. In the military, it's protocol for a lower ranking officer to salute a higher ranking one. The incompetent leader felt inferior, embarrassed, and upset, and attempted to avoid saluting his superior officer.

The competent Leader, said, "We salute the rank, not the man." This is how you can show respect to someone authentically. Recognizing their rank, their position, their responsibilities, even if their leadership abilities are lacking.

Ownership

Just like Heroic Leaders take ownership of their contribution to the company and its overall success, how we respond appropriately is also something we should take ownership of. Regardless of how others react or behave, we must decide on our response.

In the difficult conversations that did not go well, what could we learn from those? What could we have done differently? We definitely learn best when things do not go according to plan. If we did misspeak or came across differently than we desired, we need to own up to that. This gesture of goodwill is often well received, even if the other party was unreasonable. It tends to lessen the tension. I've also found that future conversations with those more difficult coworkers tended to go more smoothly after taking ownership for a misstep.

Taking ownership of our responses demonstrates a learning attitude and a growth mindset.

Patience

It can be tempting to jump into a conversation without all of the facts – an open and shut case, as they call it in the court system. But the more information that we have before coming to a conclusion and having the conversation, the better. A question like, "Can you help me understand this better?" It's not confrontational; it's inquisitive, and it's asking for their view of what happened. This earns more trust then coming in with our minds already made up. Once we have a strong, clear understanding of what did happen, we must always leave a little bit of room for the possibility that a perspective or information could be a little off. This helps clarify misunderstandings and can prevent unnecessary tension and conflict. We want to make difficult conversations as positive as possible.

Follow Through

While the conversation can be the most demanding thing, the most important part is not the conversation itself. It's the action steps as a result of that conversation. Sometimes, to avoid tension, promises are made rashly. Regardless of how the other party follows through on what they commit to, it's important for us as Heroic Leaders to hold up our end of the deal.

As I shared before in the chapter on trust, we must follow through on what we commit to in order to earn and keep trust. And if something comes up that delays or prevents us from keeping our word, we must be diligent about communicating those changes. Not with assigning blame or giving excuses, but calmly and clearly explaining what occurred and what actions we will take going forward.

Heroic Leaders choose how they will respond in any situation. The quality of our Leadership is best proven in the difficult conversations. Preparing beforehand can enable those conversations to resolve or move forward in a win-win way.

The ability to respond appropriately is a life skill, not just a professional one. Developing a reputation for appropriate responses personally and professionally will distinguish you amongst your peers and perhaps even your supervisors. Your loved ones will appreciate calm, thoughtful, win-win responses as well.

Heroic Leadership is committed to responding to others in the very best way, treating others as more important than ourselves. This is a professional life skill you can develop regardless of your role. And as you progress in your career, this will become an invaluable aspect of your engaging, effective Leadership.

Responsibility – Preparing Myself to Respond

My Next Best Steps

_____

_____

_____

Chapter 8

The Power of Story

According to a study published in the Harvard Business Review, facts, shared along with a story, are remembered 20 times better than just sharing the facts alone. No matter how compelling those facts are. But it's not just the novelty of the story or how it relates to the listener that matters. There's actually a chemical response. Wild!

When we engage with a story, multiple feel-good hormones are released. That's why bedtime stories are such a memorable event for little ones. It's not because you're reading the same book over and over and over again. It's not the words on the page. It's the experience the child has with you. It's a special time – it's quiet, it's dark, it's personal. The reason our toddlers asked us to read the same book repeatedly was not for the story itself. It was the time with us.

That helped them sleep, that released feel-good hormones. It built a bond. It helped to learn the language. It was practical, personal, and deeply meaningful.

And that's why leveraging the power of story is so important as a Heroic Leader.

There are four types of stories I want to share with you in this chapter. The first one is most important.

One Story

I may have to repeat myself in order for this next statement to have full impact on your beliefs.

There hasn't been, there isn't now, and there won't ever be another one of you.

There could be people with the same name, similar experiences and backgrounds, even identical career paths and life choices.

But you are infinitely unique. There is no one else like you.

The reason I have to repeat this in a workshop or a keynote speech is that it makes sense to us mentally. But it often doesn't impact people fully until they reflect on it for a moment.

When we believe that we are infinitely unique, truly one of a kind, it changes our perspective on what's important, on what's meaningful. For most of us, we are our toughest critics. Life, academics, sports, business, well-meaning parents, peers, and ourselves pile on, seeming to reinforce the idea that there isn't anything special or unique about us. But it's just not true.

You are one of a kind. And so are all the people around you.

That's why listening to other's stories and sharing your own is so important. When your story resonates with others, they have a chemical reaction to that story, and to you. Finding common ground, shared values, the same mission – all lead to the ability to positively influence and impact others, to make a difference in the world.

Their Story

Just as important as understanding how unique our story is, it's a game changer to deliberately ask and listen to the stories of the people around you. With the rise of technology, we're bombarded with digital attempts striving to distract and keep our attention.

When you choose to take time out from the busyness of life and zero in on the answer to the question you just asked someone, you differentiate yourself. You communicate to that person that you genuinely care about them. You're curious. You want to know more about them. And when they share their story with you, it inspires trust. So long as that story is not followed up with an ask, or a hook, or a pitch.

When was the last time someone asked you for your story? And not at a networking event where you're supposed to hear that question. But seemingly out of the blue, at random, a coworker expressed enough genuine interest in your life that they asked to know more about you - your background, your growing up years, your goals and dreams.

Some of the most effective ways to earn trust, to impact and influence others, can be the simplest. Just listening to their story is highly effective, and anyone can do it.

Try it. Follow up your initial question about their story, with some excellently worded additional questions. This proves to a greater degree that you're genuinely interested to know more about them. You're not just trying to break the ice or to gain some leverage on them. You're genuinely curious.

Genuinely curious people always have a greater impact and influence on others.

My Story

Typically, when I ask about others' life stories, and then ask some additional questions as follow up, they want to reciprocate. They also are genuinely curious about my life. I don't ask others about their lives as a gimmick to get them to ask me about my life. That's manipulative and shallow. Learning more about me helps the two of us connect better.

Make this a habit in your life -- no matter what age you are or what role you have – you will automatically make a difference in the lives of those around you. It's just so rare.

When people ask me about my life, I start off with a fairly simple explanation. I don't go too deep too quickly. I do this for two reasons: I don't want to overshare and bore them to death! The other reason is to determine if they're genuinely interested to know more. If they are, they will ask more questions.

It's not a test. It's valuing their time. If they're genuinely curious, they will invest the time to learn more. If they're not, the conversation ends with both of us having learned more about each other. Either way, it's a win-win experience.

My ultimate goal as a Heroic Leader is not to tell my story. My higher goal is to learn more about the people around me. Heroic Leaders are not focused on themselves. Heroic Leaders are more concerned about others. That's why other people's stories fascinate me.

And the ones who are genuinely curious, they ask some incredible questions to me. I get to learn about myself from some of their excellent questions. Another form of a win-win conversation.

Our Story

When I encountered the book *Building a Story Brand* by Donald Miller in 2021, I was hooked! If you have not read this book, you must. Whether you own a business, are a senior Leader in a business, or have no plans to be, it does not matter.

This book helped me tremendously in my marketing efforts, in my professional sales, in my Leadership, and in my public speaking and workshops. Donald Miller revealed the pattern behind every Hollywood blockbuster movie. And it's the key to effectively sharing the story of your company.

Here are the 7 parts to a story-driven script....

1) A hero (them, **not you!**)
2) Has a problem
3) Who encounters a guide (**you!**)
4) Who has a plan
5) When their Call To Action is executed
6) Achieves resounding success
7) Avoiding disaster

Those are the 7 steps. It does not matter whether your company provides a service, creates a product, or anything in between. Your client, colleague, loved one, company, or the community *is the hero*, **always.**

This is why it does not matter how expensive or professional or polished our advertising is. If it's heavy with features and benefits, how many years the company has been in business, or how their service or solution is the best in the whole wide world, it just doesn't resonate. Your heroes need to know how your service, product, or solution either solves their problem or gives them a competitive advantage.

The same is true for team members. They don't care how long the company has been in business. They don't care how beautiful the facilities are, or how well-stocked the break room is. They need to know whether they are an invaluable asset or not.

This is where Heroic Leadership comes in. When you understand what your coworkers, customers, vendors, and communities are looking for, you can provide it. Regardless of age, experience, role, education, or expertise, people all around you are hungry to work alongside a professional who puts them first, who knows them and what they need.

Let's say you are not in a management role in your current career step. If you work for a quality company with a positive work environment, you can become an invaluable asset to them. Not just in the quality of work that you do, but by becoming a walking billboard, actively advertising that you love where you work. You become one of the best kind of recruiters – a story brand recruiter, a highly satisfied team member, who **knows** they contribute a critical piece of the overall success.

Quality team members want to make a difference. When you share with others that you are freed and empowered to make a difference, it's the most effective way to attract and keep quality team members.

If you're searching for your next career step, look for clues like this, but not from the recruiter or human resources or senior management. Look and listen for the clues from the team members. That's the biggest giveaway on a healthy work environment.

Story. Use it wisely, use it liberally, use it consistently. You will make a difference to others, to your company, and to yourself. Every Heroic Leader has a compelling story. While you strengthen your Heroic Leadership, you inspire others to begin their Heroic Leadership journey, too.

Unleash Story – Starting with My One Story

My Next Best Steps

_____

_____

_____

Empower

Chapter 9

Equip

These next three chapters will most directly apply to people in management or Leadership roles. But the principles are good to be aware of and to practice, should you aspire to have that same kind of role in the future.

One of the most essential elements for equipping team members is trust. I know we've talked a great deal about trust in this book, but there's an aspect we haven't directly covered yet -- extending trust.

When I was seven years old, I went to a swimming party. As I was floating around on a black innertube, a boy came up for air, tugged sharply on the tube, dumping me into the pool. To this point, I had taken no swimming lessons. I swallowed a lot of water on my way to the edge of the pool. It took me many, many years to enjoy being in the water again.

When our little ones first began swimming, I had to resist the urge to grab them if I felt they had been under the water too long. I didn't want to be a helicopter parent! I didn't want to ruin their fun. So in spite of my strong concern for them, I extended trust to them. I trusted that they would know when to come up for air. And they always did.

As Heroic Leaders, we want to earn and keep trust. We also need to extend that to our team members. Just as you entrusted the car to your teenager when they drove for the first time on their own, there are ways that you can extend trust to people on your team.

One of the biggest reasons why successful, privately held companies do not sell is that ownership cannot let go of the vine. What this means is they believe they have to be directly involved in every aspect of the business – the day-to-day operations, in major decisions, in marketing and branding, and so on. Now that would seem to make sense, especially if they started the business, but this is highly counterproductive. Potential investors do not want to buy a business that is completely reliant upon the founder for its future success. They want a business that can grow and run even better after the founder has retired or started a new chapter in their life. That's one of the proofs of a successful company.

Did you know that the word "success" is built into the word "succession?" The successful transition across generations is long-term proof of the true success of a company. A sizable number of companies have remained in business for 20 or 30 years. The ones with enduring success accomplish this feat generation after generation.

When you extend trust to your team members, when you delegate with clear instructions, you're giving them the opportunity to prove their capability. While this could be scary for the one extending trust, for the one delegating, it's necessary. In order for a team to experience high performance levels, they must be entrusted with increasing responsibilities. All of the most important tasks cannot fall on the Leaders. Remember the definition for Lead? Bringing others along as someone who has gone before? You're doing it together, not alone.

John Maxwell said, "If you reach the top of the mountain alone, you're just a hiker." Don't be a hiker; be a Heroic Leader.

Setting the Standard

It's quite true to state that Ritz Carlton Hotels have set the standard for the customer experience in the hospitality industry. A rabid fan base, legendary customer service, and industry-leading occupancy have all contributed to their growing success. But that's not what's at the root of their success. There are two rules that every location implements, and they're game changers!

The first one is called the 12-foot rule. Anytime a guest is within 12 feet of any staff member, the staff member is required to greet them. "Good morning," "How is your day going?," "Welcome!" or "Are you enjoying your stay?" Every team member is entrusted with engagement.

The second rule could be a little scary in principle. Every team member is entrusted to make things right when customers have a negative experience, with a limit of $2000. Horst Schultze, the cofounder of Ritz Carlton, said that the average cost to make things right was less than $500.

Let's take a closer look at these two standing rules. They're about engagement, they're about relationship, they're about an excellent experience. In his book, *Excellence Wins*, Schultze states that there's always room at the top for excellence.

Before you object by stating that a luxury hotel can easily afford to do these things, let me reveal the results to you.

Their incredibly loyal guests will go out of their way to stay at a Ritz Carlton hotel, regardless of the commute. Their legendary stories of customer service have become viral social media content, viewed millions of times around the world. Ritz Carlton's occupancy rate is several percentage points higher than the national average, with their room rate being more than twice the national average.

Turns out, intentional engagement and empowerment leads to greater profitability. Who knew?! It shouldn't be a surprise to us that these principles work.

Let's go back to your likely objection. "John, we don't have $2,000 per issue to make things right." Understood. But it's not the amount of money; it's the empowerment of the team to make the decision on the spot. Any team member was authorized to make that call. And they would be supported by management when they did.

Is your team empowered to take initiative, fully understanding from you what is approved beforehand? If your team has to consistently check in with you to get approval for something, it automatically communicates two things: they are not empowered, and if a difficult customer wants a better deal, they simply have to get access to you and work hard enough to get it.

No matter what spending limit you choose to be acceptable, giving your bought in, trusted team members the approval in advance to solve issues will not just empower them, it will smooth the customer experience. This will retain key clients and attract more quality clients looking for the same kind of experience. Customers want speed, convenience, and companies they can trust. Empowering your team members enables you to accomplish those..

Freedom

It might seem contrary to state that clear boundaries provide freedom, but they absolutely do. Boundaries sound like restriction, like fences, like what you can't do. But when they're communicated intentionally, consistently, and with clear explanations, your team can better understand and appreciate why those boundaries are in place.

When our children were younger, they would go to a new place with toys they had never seen before. If they had too many options - seemingly unlimited choices - they would play with one toy, then see another, then see another, then see the toy that another child had. They would never settle down and play with one toy for an extended period of time.

When you give your team a well-defined set of options and explain why, they are freed to work within those boundaries. It helps them focus better. It gives them more confidence. It enables them to take initiative and problem solve more easily. It requires you as a Heroic Leader to spell those things out clearly, consistently, and in advance of situations when your team may be required to make those tough decisions.

Some of the best opportunities to remind the team is following an experience where things did not go according to plan. Rather than assigning the blame to the team member who experienced that interaction, a Heroic Leader takes responsibility for the situation, so long as it was not a repeat issue. This creates a learning opportunity for the whole team. "When this happens to you……." As the Leader, you walk through the options with them. You explain what you would approve and under what circumstances.

When your team encounters that scenario again, they'll remember the real-life example, the solutions you offered, and take appropriate action.

If you're thinking to yourself that you shouldn't take responsibility for someone else's mistake, let me share an excellent resource with you. Jocko Willink, a former Navy S.E.A.L. Team Leader, wrote an excellent book, entitled *Extreme Ownership*. One principle he shared in that book has stuck with me for many years. As I shared earlier in the book, Jocko stated that when the mission was a success, the credit went to his team. When the mission was a failure, he took responsibility.

It's easy and expected to point the finger at someone else. Heroic Leaders, on the other hand, look to equip their team and improve for the next challenge.

Continuous improvement is not necessary when everything is running smoothly. It's invaluable when things don't go according to plan.

Values

We've talked about trust, we've talked about engagement, and we've talked about giving clear boundaries. Those things can be undermined when the company values are just a slogan.

It doesn't matter how emotionally moving, how catchy or how memorable a company's values are, posted prominently throughout the business and on the website. As a Leader, you have the responsibility and the opportunity to live out and support the values of the company.

Does your company do the right thing no matter what? Does your company take the absolute best care of people inside and outside the business? Does your company genuinely care about quality and safety? Is your company genuinely committed to the success and health of its team members? Does your company conduct its business with ethics and integrity?

Do you?

That list of questions reminded me of my time working with Tim in retail. We didn't have any posters on the wall, and the employee handbook had just a few printed pages. But that didn't matter.

My experience of working with Tim - how he modeled the values of the company, alongside his own personal values - reinforced my belief that when you take the absolute best care of people, stay consistent to your values, and provide a quality service or product, it's profitable.

I have experienced this many times throughout my career. Unfortunately, my experience has been more often that the values posted on the website, on the walls, or stated in the meetings, did not align with the actual experience.

The most important aspect of empowering your team members is to be consistently true to your values. Heroic Leaders live out their values in everything they do.

The long term, profitable success of your team and your company relies on your ability to Heroically Lead by equipping those around you.

Equip – Equipping Others

My Next Best Steps

Chapter 10

Support

Remember, how the word "trust" comes from the word "truss?" Clearly, there's a connection between supporting others while earning and keeping their trust. What are some ways that Heroic Leaders achieve this?

Progress

During one of my sales calls years ago, there was an intriguing placard on the wall. It read, "Progress is the goal, not perfection." I've always remembered that slogan because it's quite true!

Perfection is not the goal; excellence is. And progress is the measurable growth on our way to achieving excellence.

In my last book, *Winning Secrets: How a Dictionary and a Ruler Can Change Your Life*, I chose to interview extraordinarily successful professionals around my home state of Ohio. During those conversations, and in my own research, I discovered that the opposite of Winning at Life was not failure. In fact, almost every person I interviewed saw failure as a part of the learning process to figure out what would work eventually. The opposite of Winning at Life is not failing; it's giving up, not trying at all.

Sometimes, team members quit on giving their best effort, because the goal, in reality by the business leaders, is perfection, rather than excellence. What a shame that someone with remarkable attendance, high quality, and a commitment to their team would be written up and publicly shamed for just one small mistake?! I've seen it happen far too many times in my career. Repeating the same mistake over and over again? That does need to be addressed. But just one mistake and their first one?

When companies fix the blame, rather than fixing the issue, they miss the opportunity to improve and help their team members grow. They communicate that perfection is the goal. It would seem reasonable that strong consequences like write ups, docking pay, or public embarrassment would get results. And they do. But not the results you're thinking. It results in a workforce that's timid, underperforming, giving just enough effort to get by.

One of the most effective ways to engage quality team members with a strong work ethic is to support them when they mess up - a genuine mistake, not a calculated, deceitful choice, but simply a genuine misstep. Other team members notice the positive reinforcement and are encouraged to give greater effort, to take initiative within boundaries, to focus on quality.

It's one thing to strive for excellence; it's another thing to try avoiding mistakes at all costs.

Which environment do you think is more supportive and more productive?

Just as babies learn to walk, or when we learn to ride a bicycle, it's tiny improvements over time that add up to walking easily and riding the bike smoothly. It just takes time. Anything of lasting quality takes time, and more time than we would like.

Do you remember Day One in your current role? Did you want to do the best work, contributing immediately to the company's success? Did you want to be exceptional at your work, even though you just started?

The learning curve always feel steeper than we think it should. Let me rephrase that: **the learning curve always feels steeper than we think it should, if we desire to achieve excellence.**

The team members who are just in it for a paycheck do not possess this inner tension. They're happy to go through the motions, doing work that's good enough to not cause problems and keep receiving their pay.

But those who aspire to Heroic impact, who are Heroic Leaders, they want to do their very best work as soon as possible. They know it will take time, and they resist the urge to impatiently rush through the process to try and get there too quickly. They know that quality takes time to build. So they trust the process. They're always learning, always improving, never settling for "just okay."

When you see team members giving this kind of effort, you need to make sure that you support them. Let them know you notice their effort. It makes a significant difference!

Viral Success

One of the downsides of social media is the illusion of "overnight" success. If you were to believe the growing number of self-described millionaires, thought leaders, or influencers, who pose in front of a mansion or around a sports car (which they may not even own!), often, these are fake projections of wealth.

My personal experience around people of significant wealth and great character is that they do not flaunt it. They leverage it. They use their wealth to grow more wealth. They give abundantly and happily to others. They're curious and hungry to learn more. They choose to set aside time for their loved ones and for their passions in life.

There is no overnight success.

All of the highly successful, famous people that we know had a difficult path on their way to fame and fortune.

How does this apply to me as a Heroic Leader? We must trust the process, for ourselves and for our team members.

One of the strongest proofs of our success as Heroic Leaders is not what we flaunt; it's what others experience firsthand with us. That's the real proof.

A Blessing

Quality organizations embrace continuous improvement as a blessing, not a burden. They understand that when they answer the question, "How can we do this better?," the answers they receive will earn them a competitive advantage.

With the pace of change faster than ever, a global marketplace, and a highly competitive workforce, companies cannot afford to do things the way they've always done them.

Heroic Leaders consistently ask this question of themselves, their team, their company, their vendors, their customer relationships, and their community impact. Rather than being a threat, this question becomes a tool for insight.

In the spring of 2020, I had the privilege of attending a business incubator in central Ohio. The guest speaker was a brilliant thought leader with a PhD in organizational change. She shared that at the beginning of the 1900's, a business could reinvent itself every 75 years and be successful. By the 1980's, the need to reinvent shortened dramatically to every 15 years. At the turn of this century, it shrunk to every 5 years.

She went on to explain that the time companies need to be looking at how they deliver their service, product, or solutions is on the upward curve of growth, not when things settle down. When companies reached the apex of growth and experienced a plateau, drifting into a slight decline, only a tenth of those companies survived. They were either bought out or went out of business.

That was back in early 2020 before the pandemic. I believe it's safe to estimate that the pace of change has only gotten faster. This doesn't mean that we need to change our values, or even what our core business solutions, products, or services are. It does mean that we must be constantly looking at **how** we deliver them to our customers and **how** we work with our teams to achieve that delivery.

This is why Heroic Leaders are essential to long-term success. Their personal standard is excellence. The question, "How can we do this better" is a way of life for them.

Look for this high-quality culture. If you don't see it intentionally within your current company, try to build it with them. If there's no interest, explore options and consider looking for a better fit. While the number is smaller, there are definitely businesses who would appreciate and value a Heroic Leader who supports a continuous improvement culture.

Support – Supporting Others

My Next Best Steps

_____

_____

_____

Chapter 11
Recognize

Multiple studies on workforce retention revealed a consistent attribute in the top three responses. They all related to company culture, a positive work environment that was engaging and communicating consistently.

But communicating what? While constructive criticism and feedback is helpful for career growth, I believe there's an even more effective tool for employee engagement. And it goes all the way back to our childhood.

In an earlier chapter, I shared with you my experience of being a summer camp counselor. There's a powerful life experience at that ranch I want to share with you that occurred over 25 years ago. And yet I remember it as clearly as the day it happened.

It was the eighth and final week of summer camp. I was exhausted. Being responsible for as many as ten 10-year-old boys for eight weeks wears a guy out! I had a newfound appreciation for my parents, that's for sure!

While the ranchers waited outside for the lunch bell to ring one day, the weary counselors and I had a few moments of peace and quiet. As I was sitting at my table, I noticed our camp director, Ralph, walking my direction. Over 6 feet tall, a handlebar mustache, and booming laugh, Ralph was an excellent summer camp director. He was also known for being direct. We never had to guess what was on Ralph's mind.

You know that look, when your supervisor gets your attention and starts to walk your way? That's what Ralph did. Inside, I was bracing myself for what I thought would be constructive criticism or feedback. But it wasn't that at all. Ralph said two sentences that have impacted my life to this day.

He said, "John, at the beginning of the summer, I wasn't sure that you would make it. But I can honestly say, you're one of the best counselors we've got." Then he turned and walked away.

Suddenly, I didn't feel so tired anymore. When I share this story as a public speaker or in a workshop, sometimes I get chills, recalling that experience. It was so emotionally powerful. I remember the color of the tables, where I was sitting - the whole scene is vividly clear in my memory. Why?

The power of recognition. When we provide positive feedback to others ***in connection with something tangible they did or achieved***, it sticks in our minds. It happens so rarely in our lives, personally or professionally.

The lifelong impact you can have on a team member, especially if you're in a Leadership role, is far bigger than you might realize.

Here are some ways to consistently spot opportunities for recognition.

V.o.C.

In the customer experience world, V.o.C. stands for Voice of the Customer. Be on the lookout for and keep track of commendations from customers specifically towards your team members. Another way is to ask some of your best customers, your raving fans, for any positive experiences they've had with your team. You're deliberately mining positive feedback so you can share it with your team members.

It's one thing to recognize someone for their attendance or their positive attitude. It's even more impactful to share how their work made a difference to the company and to its best customers.

Flip The Script

Another powerful way to employ recognition is to Flip The Script on them. Here's what I mean. **Not** at the annual review or when it's expected, say to a high performing bought in team member, "John, I need to talk to you in my office for a minute."

Did you feel it? That sinking feeling inside, like you're about to get written up for something? That's likely how most people feel when they hear their supervisor say that to them.

As they cautiously enter your office and sit down, they're bracing themselves - like I was with Ralph - internally expecting to hear constructive criticism or ways to improve or a major mistake they made. Instead....

You share with them, "I spoke with Mr. Smith, one of our best customers, and he says that every time he works with you, he receives what he needs, when he needs it, with the quality he expects. I wanted to thank you for providing excellent customer experience. He's one of our best clients.

It makes an enormous difference in the success of our business."

Give them a moment or two to recover from the shock of not being reprimanded, then follow up with a question.

"Is there anything we could do to help you do your job even better so you can continue providing that level of service to others?"

Then you stop talking, grab a pen and paper, and prepare to write. Even if you have a photographic memory, it's important that your bought-in team member sees you writing down their answer.

One word of massive caution here: you have to close the loop. If you write down their suggestion and do nothing with it, it would be far better simply to compliment them and move on. If you're going to ask for their feedback, for their help, you've got to look into their idea and close the loop by sharing the results with them. Whether you can implement their suggestion or not, following up with what you learned, what you can or cannot do, and thanking them for their input, will encourage them to do more of it.

Odds are good, that if they notice a source of friction for customers, it's likely happening to more than just the customers they're responsible for.

By pairing recognition with asking for their help, you are supporting quality, bought-in team members more than you might realize.

They now know, with certainty, that they're making a difference. The quality of their work is contributing to the overall success of the company. They have no doubt of that. The bought-in team members want the company to continue to improve, because they have an ownership mindset. Because they aspire for excellence and assume the company does, too.

R.A.E.

Another excellent way to recognize team members is what I call Random Acts of Encouragement. For a couple of years, I was the director of business development for a small company in central Ohio, about 15 employees total.

From day one, I made a personal commitment to encourage every single team member. I made a note on my calendar, so I wouldn't forget to leave a handwritten note on each person's desk one day of each month. Just a sentence or two, recognizing them for their contribution to the success of the company, or their commitment to customer service - a variety of things. I did this consistently for two years. When I left for a new opportunity, I discovered something incredible.

One department of our company was a contact center that provided service for our clients' customers. The two ladies in that department had incredible soft skills over the phone. Every month, I would encourage them by recognizing their abilities and empathetic customer service. I knew what high quality phone-based service looked like, because I had achieved excellent results in a Fortune 10 contact center.

When I left, I learned that those two ladies had kept every.single.note. I wrote to them. 24 notes in all. That's how much my encouraging words meant to them.

I highly recommend doing this for team members, either by writing notes that you leave for them to discover or through voicemails. Emails feel too businesslike, and text messages can lack that personal touch. That's why I prefer handwritten notes if they work in the same office. If you don't work in the same location, leaving a voicemail is also good because they can hear the tone in your voice.

Reward

A few years ago, I read an article on a customer experience website that highlighted a unique employee rewards program for a home building company. They called it The Golden Nail. On every team member's desk, there was a wooden stand, painted bright gold, with five holes in it. Every time a team member received positive feedback from customers or contributed an idea that improved quality or reduced cost for the company, they received a Golden Nail. Once they collected five Golden Nails, they received their choice of reward: a gift card, company swag, paid time off, etc. Along with the gift, a companywide communication shared what that team member had done, and how they had contributed to the overall success.

Not surprisingly, the morale of the company was extremely high, as well as their customer experience levels. That's the power of recognition and rewarding it. But not just with money or a gift, but with good publicity as well. It reinforces company values and encourages others to contribute in the same way.

One reason I admire the employee-owned companies is that team members know their quality contribution increases the profitability of the company, which, in turn, enlarges their profit share at the end of the year. It's truly a win-win model.

For one year, I had the privilege of working for TMC Transportation, a flatbed trucking company based in Des Moines, Iowa. The company had beautiful tractors, – black late model Peterbilt's, with twin, shiny smokestacks, exceptionally clean. While working for this company, I discovered that they were employee owned.

While not a guarantee, I have found that ESOPs, as they're called, tend to have higher quality, stronger attendance, higher morale, and stronger profitability than most companies. And that makes sense. When team members know that their efforts make a difference, it's good to reward those positive choices.

Retain

In today's highly competitive workforce, companies not only need to hire quality team members, they need to keep them as well. Here are three ideas on how to achieve that through recognition.

I've worked for several companies that stated they had an open-door policy. If I had a concern, I could share that openly with leadership.

At one company, this was true at the beginning of my time there. But a couple of years in, the culture shifted. Toxic leaders were kept in leadership, and toxic team members were kept on staff, resulting in promising younger team members and long-term customers leaving us. I left a couple of years later to pursue my own endeavors. What I had thought could be an extremely rewarding, enjoyable career for many years ended up being a career step that lasted just 4 years.

Having an open door is not nearly as important as having open ears, open eyes, and an open mind.

Just because the door is open does not mean that constructive feedback is welcomed. As a Heroic Leader, you have the incredible opportunity to significantly impact the work environment and the culture of your company. One of the most effective ways to achieve that is to offer, model, and support open communication. Quality team members can spot authentic openness and actively look for it.

A Gallup poll showed that nearly 90% of team members want training and development. But there's a catch - they want training and development that helps them grow personally and professionally, not necessarily just for promotions, an expanding career path, or for improved technical skills. The same survey revealed that team members prefer a coaching style of Leadership versus a management style. What's the difference?

I recently completed a ChatGPT exercise to highlight the difference between Consulting and Coaching. I provide business coaching, not consulting. I wanted to understand the differences between the two.

Simply put, consultants typically work through the data, while coaches focus on developing the relationships.

A management style versus a coaching style is quite similar. Management is often focused on running the business well, on sound business practices, while business coaching is designed to help the team members achieve their greatest potential.

One is about efficiency, while the other is more about growth.

Some of the best business Leaders in my life were ones who viewed their role as a coach more than a manager. When I reflect on my years as an immature leader, I realized I was attempting to manage people, not to coach them. Sometimes, I would coach others, but it was occasionally, not consistently.

As a current or aspiring Heroic Leader, you have the opportunity to bring out the best in others. By recognizing their strengths, their skills, and their potential, you automatically help the people around you accomplish more in life. Effective coaches are Heroic Leaders because they bring others along on a path they've been on before, with the goals of achieving excellence and having a positive impact on others.

This might sound quite lofty, but the odds are fairly good that you may already be doing this. As a parent, as a spouse or life partner, as an older sibling, as a teammate - you may already be having more impact than you know.

Remember the story at the beginning of this chapter, the one I shared about Ralph and his encouraging feedback? When Ralph shared those two sentences with me, he didn't know that my experience would stay fresh in my mind decades later. He simply acted on what he saw and decisively shared feedback with me.

We all have the opportunity to do that. If encouraging others is a daily priority, you'll be looking for the windows of opportunity to recognize others.

We never know the second- or third-degree impact that our words can have on others. Those words that Ralph shared with me have directly impacted tens of thousands of people by now. One of my personal goals is to impact and influence over 1 million people within the next decade. How incredible that two sentences from a man who acted on what he saw over 25 years ago will lead to the indirect encouragement of millions.

The same opportunity for massive impact is available to you as well.

Recognize – Unleash the Power of Recognition

My Next Best Steps

_____

_____

_____

Become

Chapter 12
Becoming a Heroic Leader

Authentic

It all started with a happy birthday wish on LinkedIn.

Every day, through social media, I personally celebrate my first-degree connections' birthdays. A little while back, a business coach in Switzerland opened a conversation with me in response to my genuine happy birthday wish.

Over time, our relationship grew into a strongly positive, affirming friendship. One of the personal insights I gained from my time with Markus Neukom was identifying and overcoming Imposter Syndrome.

This silent parasite eats away at confidence, authenticity, and the drive to achieve our BHAG's. My discussions with Markus revealed how I subconsciously perceived myself, which came through in my conversations, my marketing, my sales efforts, my close relationships, and my self-talk.

Every aspect of my life was touched by this inaccurate, subtle saboteur.

Even more fascinating, to me, is that Imposter Syndrome most often impacts high achievers. To all appearances, these self-motivated, highly driven individuals have achieved measurable success, major life and career goals, and developed relationships with other high achieving people.

But they tend to hit an invisible, glass ceiling, where they can clearly see where their potential lies, but they just can't seem to get there. That's where unveiling imposter syndrome becomes key.

In order to be fully authentic, we need to fully believe in our worth, our potential, and our value to others. As I mentioned earlier, Tony Robbins said that the golden ticket of influence has shifted away from NLP – Neuro Linguistic Programming – to authenticity. The wonderful thing about authenticity is that it cannot be faked indefinitely. Time reveals whether someone is authentic or simply skilled at projecting an image of authenticity to others.

If you wrestle with the fact that you've accomplished a great deal in your life but feel like you're not living up to your full potential, I highly recommend following Markus Neukom on LinkedIn. His content is powerfully encouraging.

If you're just beginning your pursuit of Heroic Leadership, you have the opportunity to build on truth from respected mentors, thought leaders, and other Heroic Leaders in your life. Borrow their confidence, borrow their belief in you. Believe in the truth they're sharing with you and take action on your next best steps.

If you're confused or unsure whether you're being confident or projecting it, ask a truth teller that you trust for their input.

The more authentic you can be with yourself and others, the greater impact you will have on others.

Confident

For most of my life, I projected confidence. Internally, I was too concerned about others' opinions of me, perceptions that I perceived falsely or their opinions that truly existed. My obsession with earning others' approval eroded my confidence.

I wrestled with the paradox of being a confident man who did not desire to be arrogant towards others. Because of my religious upbringing, I knew that pride was wrong. So how does a Heroic Leader display confidence without being arrogant?

It goes back to our belief. Not just belief in ourselves, but in our purposes, in life, in the positive impact we have on others, in the difference we make wherever we go. This is why adding a mentor is so important.

In 2019, I added a business mentor to my life. Ken's respectable achievements, career, and values resonated strongly with me. His wise counsel and actionable input helped me progress significantly in my professional pursuits.

I also gained personally from my time with Ken. Relying on his confidence in me strengthened me to put in the work to achieve my BHAGs. It wasn't overnight success, that's for sure! But it absolutely resulted in measurable progress.

If you would benefit from an increase in genuine confidence, find someone you trust and borrow their confidence in you. As you learn from them and do the work necessary, you will grow in your own genuine confidence.

Results gained through hard work result in greater confidence.

There's no shortcut to this. The highly successful, wealthy businesspeople in my life have a quiet confidence. They don't need to be loud, flashy, or talking all about what they've achieved. Their results speak for themselves.

Contrast that with people who are loudly declaring their success and displaying high dollar possessions as proof.

Strong confidence does not require possessions as proof of success.

Neither does Heroic Leadership.

Your title, your income, the number of people who report to you, your responsibilities – none of those are clear indicators of Heroic Leadership. It's more subtle than that.

Heroic Leadership is about increasing our capacity to bring others along as someone who has been there before, with the goals of excellence and benefiting others as a life goal.

Those who are supremely confident know who they're influencing and impacting, as well as the goals they have achieved. That's why highly successful people become well known "all of a sudden." It took time for them to earn the results necessary. Their confidence in themselves and in the process is what made their high level of success a reality.

Coachable

It should not be surprising to us that some of the most effective thought leaders, consultants, and coaches have coaches of their own. The best athletes in the world rely on coaches to improve their performance.

Whether you hire a coach for business or life or not, it's not as important as the attitude of ***being coachable***. This is where pride sabotages potential and opportunity. Hubris is why so many promising companies and ideas have failed. Because leaders became uncoachable.

Regardless of our experience, age, or achievements, there will *always* be someone we can learn from.

During job interviews, the interviewer would ask me, "What's your greatest weakness?"

My response to that was always, "What I don't know. That's why I've committed myself to always learning."

There's a wealth of wisdom available all around us. A coachable spirit looks for the opportunity to learn from others. No matter where you are in your Leadership journey, you will always have greater positive impact and influence on others, if you remain coachable.

As a business coach, I look for this key attribute in a prospective client. If they're not coachable and not open to innovative ideas, it will be a waste of both of our time and their money.

One word of caution: the difference between being coachable and looking for a shortcut to success can be hard to notice. One insight I discovered is that a coachable person understands it will take time to achieve results. An impatient, immature person seeks the shortest, easiest path to success.

But that path doesn't exist.

The people with the greatest wisdom to share are deliberately cautious in who they share their insights with.

If you have a coachable attitude, are willing to put in the work for longer than you think it will take, and maintain a positive attitude, there's an abundance of wise, successful mentors and coaches willing to happily share their best practices with you.

That's a game changer for Heroic Leaders.

Courageous

When I was in high school, one of the literature books I read was *The Red Badge of Courage* by Stephen Crane. Set in the American Civil War era, the story was about an incredibly young soldier fighting for the Federal army, or the Union. During his first encounter with the enemy, the young man ran in fear. During his time away from the battlefront, he realized that he must face his fears in order to have courage. Armed with that new knowledge, he returned to the front and inspired other young soldiers to join him.

Courage is not achieved by knowledge. It's gained by experience.

My time in the military was extremely helpful for my personal development. Because I was forced to work through my fears, my challenges, and overcome my limitations, I grew in personal courage.

There's a direct correlation between courage and confidence. As I grew in confidence, I also grew in courage. As I became more courageous, I began to seek growth opportunities in my career and as a Leader.

The good news is that military experience is not required to grow in courage. Taking decisive action towards your next best step, especially outside of your comfort zone, requires courage. You may not be facing an enemy on the other side of a battlefield, but it requires courage to deliberately choose a new path, a different path than most.

Courage is required to escape the velvet trap of comfort.

Because we want to impact and influence others, to make a difference in the world, it will require courage.

Nothing of great value was achieved comfortably.

When most of your friends or colleagues have decided to settle for a comfortable life, your choice for a more difficult path requires courage. It's not the same thing as choosing something different just to be different. You have specific goals in mind. You want to make a difference in the world.

You want to impact and influence others. You want to bring others along on your journey to significant success.

All those life goals require courage. Heroism requires it. Individuals and companies who have achieved excellence are extremely exceptional. Extra ordinary effort requires courage to go against the grain, to not conform to the mainstream, typical experience.

Confident courage is infectious.

As you grow in courage, the ones you're impacting will grow as well. They'll borrow your courage just as they borrow your confidence.

Abundance

I do not mean wealth. I'm referring to an abundance mindset. I know extremely wealthy people who are miserably unhappy and possess a scarcity mindset. I have seen people in tremendous poverty exhibit remarkable generosity. An abundance mindset is not connected to our possessions. Let me share an illustration with you.

If you put seven bowls of food in front of seven puppy dogs, chaos erupts! Every puppy wants all the food in their dish and all the food in every other dish, even though they can't fit it all in their tiny bellies. That's a scarcity mindset.

Now, place those same seven bowls of food in front of seven old dogs. Those dogs each eat their food calmly, peacefully. No chaos. Why?

They know there's another meal coming. They've learned to trust their owner.

An abundance mindset is an approach to life that realizes there will always be more opportunities than any one of us can possibly achieve, and that more opportunities will come our way. The pie is so enormous that even if I double my "slice," there's still a mind-blowing amount of pie left for others, too – plenty to go around.

An abundance mindset realizes that time, relationships, opportunities, and insights are more important than money, fame, or power.

Scarcity mindset tries to avoid loss at all costs. An abundance mindset looks for Win-Win gain by working with others.

Collaboration more than competition.

That doesn't mean that abundance mindset people aren't competitive. But they're most often highly competitive with themselves, not towards others. They understand that ***they*** are the ones getting in the way of greater achievements, fruitful relationships, timely opportunities, and stronger impact.

An abundance mindset looks to tap into the unlimited opportunity in the universe. And works to share those opportunities with other abundance minded people.

A scarcity mindset works to accumulate or experience as much as possible without a regard for others. Scarcity reveals itself in people with wealth and people in poverty.

The difference between abundance mindset and scarcity mindset is two things: focus and priorities.

With just a few questions, I can discover what's most important to people and where they're focused. My years of networking have refined my ability to perceive the mindset of others. By asking a few well-worded questions, I can confirm whether my perception of their mindset is accurate. There are clues in how people talk, present themselves, and behave towards others that can indicate whether they possess a scarcity or abundance mindset.

How about you? How do you view life? I'm not talking about optimism or pessimism, the glass half empty or the glass half full. I'm talking about opportunity, potential, and purpose in life.

I was an eternal optimist for many years of my life. But I did not possess an abundance mindset until a few years ago. Here's what brought about that shift.

In 2019, a dear friend, named Pat Gano, helped me identify that my life purpose is to encourage others. No matter what form it takes – public speaking, workshop facilitation, writing books, business coaching, one-on-one conversations –I am most fulfilled when I identify what is true in people's lives and build them up on that truth. That's encouragement.

Courage is based on experience and truth, not theory and feelings.

When I clearly understood ***why*** I am here on this earth, it unlocked an awareness that I could make a difference in the world, that I could positively impact and influence others. I've been told countless times that I have the gift of encouragement.

As I began to intentionally use this gift to encourage others, I realized that the opportunity was limitless. Almost everyone desires to be encouraged, to be recognized, to be loved.

Abundance is not about results. Abundance is about opportunity.

What are you gifted at? What have people told you repeatedly is a skill you possess that comes easily or naturally to you? What did you learn and apply yourself diligently to improve?

Do you know what your purpose in life is? I didn't discover this insight until I was in my 40s. There's no need to rush into a hasty decision to determine your life purpose nor to wait in pursuing Heroic Leadership until you figure that out.

Choosing to embrace a life of abundance will automatically distinguish you amongst others. It's a highly attractive quality to others who possess the same outlook on life, who are coachable, who desire to make a difference in the world. When you consciously choose to pursue a life of abundance, you will encounter a growing number of people who desire the same thing.

The synergy of working together with other abundance minded Heroic Leaders is incredible. That opportunity is available to anyone who will embrace abundance.

Embracing Change

I recently did an exercise with ChatGPT to identify the qualities of entrepreneurial people. As a business coach, I realized that my best clients were those who had an entrepreneurial approach to their business. They heavily focused on growth, they had clear long-term goals, they executed the next best steps, and their identity was not tied up in the business itself. They intended to grow the business to sell it, transition away from it, or pass it along to the next generation.

After several hours of research, I discovered the top attribute for entrepreneurial people – embracing change.

As I shared earlier in the book, the pace of change has never been faster. And when I say embracing change, I do not mean the unwise, hasty reaction of changing things simply to change things. That's just as damaging as doing nothing at all. Doing the wrong thing because it's different is no better than staying the same.

This is why continuous improvement is an invaluable trait for Heroic Leaders. By continually asking the question, "How can we do this better?," continuous innovation and creativity are unlocked.

It does not require Heroic Leadership, or leadership at all, to stay in the same rut. It does require Heroic Leadership to make decisive, informed decisions to change course.

One question I ask to help determine if a business or business owner is entrepreneurial sounds like this: "What was the last thing you changed within your business and why?" If they cannot provide an answer to that question, they do not have a culture that embraces change.

Getting personal, let me ask you the same question: "What was the last thing *you* changed in your business or your life, and why?"

Tiny changes can lead to massive results.

Just half a degree off on the compass, over the course of thousands of miles, results in entirely different destinations. That's why navigation is far more important than takeoff and landing for successful flight. Yes, we don't want the plane to crash! But the purpose of a flight is to get from one destination to the next. Without precise navigation, that doesn't happen.

Throughout our lives, we should be making slight, intentional adjustments to stay on track with our BHAGs. That's the kind of change I'm talking about. Not massive, historic adjustments. Those happen once in a long while. The simple brilliance behind Heroic impact is the almost imperceptible adjustments that come from a strongly held belief in the value of continuous improvement. Always better. Always better than yesterday. Never settling for good enough.

That kind of change, every day, over time, changes the world.

Becoming – Qualities of a Heroic Leader

My Next Best Steps

_____

_____

_____

Chapter 13
The Ultimate Proof

In this book, we've discovered new insights on what Leadership is, and what Heroism is, along with a number of strategies to grow as Heroic Leaders.

But what's the ultimate proof of a Heroic Leader's impact and influence?

It's not age, it's not experience, it's not how many people work for you. As a parent, I have not achieved the ultimate proof of this yet. As a military leader, I did not achieve it. But as a business coach, I did. Let me share the ultimate proof of a Heroic Leader through a personal story.

I was speaking multiple times at a conference in Denver a few years ago. In exchange for presenting these sessions, I received exhibition space. After one of the sessions, a business owner approached me at my booth.

Jesse and her husband owned a successful home services business. She asked me, "Have you considered doing business coaching? I really enjoyed your sessions."

I told her that I was considering it for the following year. She then stated, "Well, I'm interested. I'd like to work with you this year."

Anytime someone tells you they would like to start working with you, the answer is always "Yes!"

For more than a year, I had the privilege of working with Jesse. She was my best coaching client because of three factors: an entrepreneurial spirit, a positive attitude, and swift execution.

Her entrepreneurial spirit meant that she and her husband already had their 10-year goal in mind, clearly defined. Growth of the business was all designed to successfully grow and exit the company in the next 10 years.

Her positive attitude, brilliant smile, infectious personality, and indomitable will to win was inspiring and refreshing.

And when we agreed on next best steps, she ruthlessly executed the game plan. Over the course of the year, we tackled employee experience, customer experience, sales opportunities, marketing strategies, social media growth, effective collaborations, and engaging training and onboarding, to name a few. In all of these ideas, Jesse was eager to explore them together, determine the next best step, and then take decisive action on that step. Every week, we would update each other on our mutual progress towards our BHAGs.

But that wasn't the ultimate proof of Heroic Leadership for me.

About nine months into our time working together, I encouraged Jesse to explore coaching other business owners in her industry because of her enduring success, positive attitude, ability to execute, and inspiring Leadership.

I was so excited to see her secure a speaking position at the very same conference I spoke at in Denver – where we met for the first time. I was even happier for her when she began to secure business coaching clients of her own.

The ultimate proof of Heroic Leadership is succession – equipping Heroic Leaders to the point that they're able to begin developing Heroic Leaders as well.

Third generation Heroic Leadership – that's the ultimate proof.

And that's why it takes so much time for the ultimate proof to emerge as a parent – it takes a couple of generations to become evident. How my grandchildren impact and influence the world is the ultimate proof of our investment – my wife and I - as a parent into our children.

The same is true for us in the business world. However, we have the distinct advantage of seeing this kind of ultimate proof far sooner.

And it doesn't require a traditional default leadership role to achieve it. In fact, there are many leaders in default roles who will not experience the ultimate proof of Leadership, because they do not engage or equip others. Their growth goals are solely for themselves.

If you have deliberately, consistently poured into others to the point that they begin pouring into others, too, that's the ultimate proof.

Experience doesn't matter. Seniority doesn't matter. Your role within the company doesn't matter. Your education doesn't matter.

The lasting, positive impact on the people you Heroically Lead, that matters. That makes a difference in the world.

Your next best step to experience the ultimate proof of Heroic Leadership is to intentionally look for the people around you who are hungry to learn, who are coachable, who desire to be encouraged and equipped. Pour into those people, and inspire them to Heroically Lead others, too.

That's how anyone can be a courageous Leader. That's how Heroic Leaders change the world.

The Ultimate Proof – Heroic Leadership Succession

My Next Best Steps

_____

_____

_____

Coming Next!

I already have the next two topics for future books in mind. But I don't know which one I'm going to publish in the fall of 2025.

Here are the two topics at play:

--The power of clarity

--Seizing opportunity

If my books have been a source of encouragement and empowerment for you, there are a few ways we can remain connected.

Follow me on social media: LinkedIn and YouTube. You can find me on both of these channels by searching my full name: John D. Hanson.

Sign up for my email newsletter that comes out three times per week, about Winning at Life – Winning Secrets.

Drop me a note. Whether by email or through social media, I love to hear how my writing, speaking, or social media content has encouraged you. It makes my day when I hear back from readers, connections, or viewers of my content.

Whether you reach out to engage or diligently follow my work, I'm grateful for receiving your most precious resource – your attention. By choosing to invest your time with me, you have given your ultimate support: your time and attention.

Thank you.

Now let's make a difference in the world together.

Let's Win More at Life as Heroic Leaders.

Bibliography

Pg. 126: https://www.dominican.edu; May 2015, "Study highlights strategies for achieving goals"

Pg. 135: The Zendesk Customer Experience Trends Report 2019, Zendesk

Pg. 171: https://www.harvardbusiness.org/what-makes-storytelling-so-effective-for-learning/

Pg. 178: Miller, Donald. *Building a Story Brand: Clarify Your Message So Your Customers Will Listen*. HarperCollins, 2017

Pg. 219: Hilgers, Laura (2023, April). "Boomers, Zoomers, Gen X, and Millennials: When It Comes to Learning, One Size Doesn't Fit All." LinkedIn Talent Blog. https://www.linkedin.com/business/talent/blog/learning-and-development/boomers-zoomers-gen-x-millennials-learning-styles

Made in the USA
Columbia, SC
17 March 2025